# *More* CYCLING *without* TRAFFIC:
## SOUTHWEST

### Nick Cotton

DIAL
HOUSE

*Front cover:* The Forest of Dean trail is one of the best in the region.

*Title page:* Easy cycling in the Forest of Dean.

*This page:* Along the riverside path between Bristol and Pill.

First published 2002

ISBN 0 7110 2871 0

© Nick Cotton 2002

Published by Dial House

an imprint of Ian Allan Publishing Ltd,
Hersham, Surrey KT12 4RG.

Printed by Ian Allan Printing Ltd,
Hersham, Surrey KT12 4RG.

Code: 0203/D

More and more people are realising that cycling is good for both health and well-being. The Government has started showing a real interest in promoting cycling as a way of solving transport problems and the National Cycle Network will soon have a major effect on helping to change lifestyles and people's mode of transport. However, vehicle numbers are still increasing which means that even minor lanes can become busy with traffic – you can very rarely be guaranteed to find the safety, peace and quiet that are the essential ingredients of a family bike ride on the road network.

This book describes 30 routes, many of them easy and waymarked, where you can cycle away from traffic, and gives further information about where to ride and how to obtain cycling leaflets produced by local authorities and other organisations.

The creek at Pill, west of Bristol.

# KEY MAP

### The Main Routes

1. From Redbrook to Bigsweir in the Wye Valley
2. The Forest of Dean
3. Gloucester & Sharpness Canal
4. Nailsworth to Stroud Railway Path
5. Cotswold Water Park
6. The Old Severn Bridge
7. Bristol to Pill beneath the Clifton Suspension Bridge
8. Leigh Woods and Ashton Court, Bristol
9. Chippenham to Calne along the National Cycle Network
10. The Ridgeway from Overton Hill to Barbury Castle
11. The Tarka Trail from Braunton to Barnstaple
12. Dunster Woods, Exmoor
13. The Quantocks Ridge, west of Bridgwater
14. The Willow Walk, near Glastonbury
15. The Grand Western Canal, Tiverton
16. Abbeyford Woods, Okehampton
17. Meldon Viaduct to Lake Viaduct, Dartmoor
18. The Military Loop Road, south of Okehampton
19. Bellever Forest, Dartmoor
20. Exe Valley through Exeter
21. Exmouth to Budleigh Salterton
22. Cardinham Woods, near Bodmin
23. Portreath to Devoran Mineral Tramroad (Redruth)
24. St Austell to Mevagissey
25. Ringstead Bay to West Lulworth
26. Affpuddle Heath Forestry, east of Dorchester
27. Wareham Forest
28. Moors Valley Country Park, west of Ringwood
29. New Forest (Linford Circuit) northeast of Ringwood
30. The New Forest Railway Path near Burley

MINEHEAD
11
BARNSTAPLE
C
16
OKEHAMPTON
EXETER
17
18
20
19
WADEBRIDGE
A
22
BODMIN
B
PLYMOUTH
ST. AUSTELL
24
REDRUTH
23
Southwest
Key
Town / City
1 to 30 Routes
A to J Other Suggested Routes

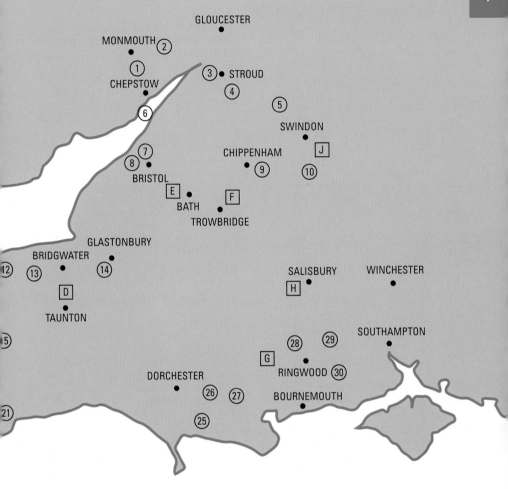

**Other suggested routes on well-known traffic-free trails (covered in *Cycling Without Traffic: Southwest*)**

A. Camel Trail (Padstow-Wadebridge-Bodmin-Poley's Bridge)
B. The Plym Valley Trail (Laira Bridge, Plymouth to Clearbrook)
C. The Tarka Trail (Barnstaple-Bideford-Great Torrington-Petrockstowe)
D. The Bridgwater & Taunton Canal Towpath
E. Bristol & Bath Railway Pathway
F. Kennet & Avon Canal Towpath (Bath-Bradford upon Avon-Devizes)
G. Castleman Trail (southwest of Wimborne Minster)
H. Ridge Routes around Wilton, west of Salisbury
J. The Marlborough to Chiseldon Railway Path

The first volume of *Cycling Without Traffic: Southwest* proved to be so popular that it seemed a good idea to produce a second volume with a further 30 traffic-free rides covering this area of the country. In the time that has elapsed between researching the first and second volumes many local authorities have produced high-quality traffic-free routes, often in conjunction with Sustrans, the engineering charity based in Bristol which was awarded £42.5 million by the National Lottery in 1995 to create the National Cycle Network. See below for more details.

**The trails can be divided into four categories:**

## 1. DISMANTLED RAILWAYS

The vast majority of Britain's railway system was built in the 50 years from 1830 to 1880. After the invention of the car and the development of the road network from the turn of the 20th century onwards, the railways went into decline and in the 1960s many of the lines were closed and the tracks lifted. This was the famous 'Beeching Axe'. It is a great tragedy that Dr Beeching was not a keen leisure cyclist! Had he set in motion the development of leisure trails along the course of the railways he was so busy closing then we could boast one of the finest recreational cycling networks in the world.

As it is, many of the railways were sold off in small sections to adjacent landowners and the continuity of long sections of dismantled track was lost. Almost 40 years on, some local authorities have risen to the challenge and created some fine trails along the course of the dismantled railways. Within this book the Stroud Valleys Trail, sections of the Forest of Dean routes and the Chippenham to Calne Trail are all good examples. The first *Cycling Without Traffic: Southwest* covered other popular railway paths in the region such as the Camel Trail in Cornwall, the Plym Valley Trail north of Plymouth, the Tarka Trail in North Devon and the Bristol & Bath Railway Path.

Mention should also be made of the developing network of cycle trails along the old mineral tramways in Cornwall. A route crossing the county from coast to coast (from Portreath, near Redruth, to Devoran, Route 23) has recently been completed.

To find out what your own local authority intends to do in the future about cycle trails in your area, contact your county council/city council/district council (see 'Local Authorities' Telephone Numbers and Websites' on page 110). Alternatively, if you wish to get involved on a national level, contact Sustrans, the organisation building the 10,000-mile National Cycle Network which will be completed in the year 2005. Its address is: Sustrans, PO Box 21, Bristol BS99 2HA (Tel: 0117 929 0888). Or try Sustrans' website at www.nationalcyclenetwork.org.uk

## 2. FORESTRY COMMISSION LAND

There are only two major Forestry Commission holdings in the area covered by this book, namely the New Forest and the Forest of Dean, although there are also many smaller woodlands, some with waymarked rides and others where it is easy to devise your own. As a general rule, it is permissible to cycle on the hard forestry tracks in woodland owned by the Forestry Commission. The chapter on the Forestry Commission (see page 104) gives details of addresses and phone numbers of regional offices so that you can find out the exact regulations (which may change at any time due to logging operations).

## 3. CANAL TOWPATHS

The British Waterways Board undertook a national survey of its 2,000 miles of towpath to see what percentage was suitable for cycling. Unfortunately, the results were not very encouraging – only about 10% meet the specified requirements.

*Right:* The Grand Western Canal in the heart of rural Devon.

The rest are too narrow, too rutted, too overgrown or pass under too many low bridges. In certain cases regional waterboards have co-ordinated with local authorities and the Countryside Agency to improve the towpaths for all users. It is to be hoped that this collaboration continues and extends throughout the country.

Cycling along canal towpaths can provide plenty of interest – wildlife, barges and locks – and the gradient tends to be flat. However, even the best-quality towpaths are not places to cycle fast as they are often busy with anglers and walkers and it is rare that cycling two abreast is feasible.

The chapter on canals (see page 106) gives you details of the Waterways Boards to contact for further information about the towpaths near to you.

The four most important canals in the region are the Gloucester & Sharpness, running southwest from Gloucester, the Kennet & Avon which runs from Bath to Reading, the Bridgwater & Taunton which links those two towns and the Grand Western, to the north of Tiverton in Devon. All four are used in part or in full in the National Cycle Network. Mention should also be made of the canals running north from Newport in South Wales which have been developed to a very high standard and also form part of the National Cycle Network.

## 4. GREAT RIDGE RIDES, OTHER BYWAYS AND BRIDLEWAYS

The Southwest is blessed with many long chalk ridges which can offer some fine off-road cycling in the summer. These rides are tougher than those along railway paths and canal towpaths and should only be undertaken on mountain bikes after a few dry days in summer. There are hundreds of miles of tracks in Wiltshire and Dorset, the most famous of which is the Ridgeway which runs from near Avebury to the Thames at Goring. Also included is the fine Quantocks Ridge with its magnificent views out over the Bristol Channel and several

*Left:* It's always useful to carry a map with you.

other enjoyable stretches of the Rights of Way network where you have a legal right to ride.

## OTHER CYCLE ROUTES

If you wish to venture beyond the relatively protected world of cycle trails, there are three choices: buy a guidebook covering mountain bike rides or rides on the lane network, write away for leaflets produced by local authorities (details of how to obtain these are given on page 108), or devise your own route.

Should you choose the third option, study the relevant Ordnance Survey Landranger map: the yellow roads criss-crossing the countryside represent the smaller, quieter lanes. When cycling off-road you must stay on legal rights of way: it is illegal to cycle on footpaths, but you are allowed to use bridleways, byways open to all traffic (BOATs) and roads used as public paths (RUPPs). These are all marked on Ordnance Survey maps. Devising routes 'blind' can sometimes be a bit of a hit-or-miss affair, however. Some tracks may turn out to be very muddy and overgrown or no more than an imaginary line across a ploughed field! It often takes several outings to devise the best possible off-road route that starts right from your front door. Expect the riding conditions to change radically from the height of summer to the depths of winter.

### THE COUNTRY CODE

- Enjoy the countryside and respect its life and work.
- Guard against all risk of fire.
- Fasten all gates.
- Keep your dogs under close control.
- Keep to rights of way across farmland.
- Use gates and stiles to cross fences, hedges and walls.
- Leave livestock, crops and machinery alone.
- Take your litter home.
- Help to keep all water clean.
- Protect wildlife, plants and trees.
- Take special care on country roads.
- Make no unnecessary noise.

Bicycles should be thoroughly overhauled on a regular basis but there are certain things worth checking before each ride, and knowledge of how to mend a puncture is essential.

**The four most important things to check are:**

1. Do both the front and rear brakes work effectively?
2. Are the tyres inflated hard?
3. Is the chain oiled?
4. Is the saddle the right height? (Low enough when sitting in the saddle to be able to touch the ground with your toes; high enough to have your leg almost straight when you are pedalling.)

Other clickings, grindings, gratings, crunchings, rattling, squeakings, wobblings and rubbings either mean that your bike needs oiling and parts need adjusting, or a trip to your local bike mechanic is long overdue. Try to give a bike shop as much warning as possible; do not expect to turn up and have your bike fixed on the spot.

## MENDING A PUNCTURE
You will need:
- a spanner to undo the nuts holding the wheel to the frame.
- tyre levers to ease the tyre off the rim.
- glue and patches.
- a pump.
- a spare inner tube.

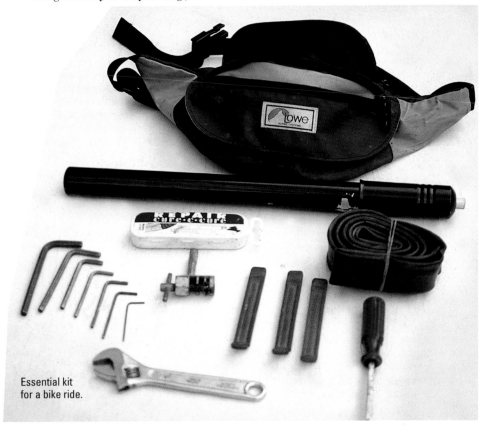

Essential kit
for a bike ride.

The items displayed on the left should always be carried, even on short rides, as walking with a bike with a flat tyre is not much fun. If you are carrying a spare inner tube, follow instructions 1-3 then 9-10.

1. Remove the wheel which has the puncture, using a spanner to undo the nuts on the hub if it is not fitted with quick-release levers (you will probably have to unhitch the brake cable in order to remove the wheel).

2. Remove the tyre from the rim, using tyre levers if the fit is tight. Insert two levers under the rim and a few inches apart and push on them together to free the tyre from the rim, taking care not to pinch the inner tube. Work the levers around the rim until the tyre is completely free.

3. Remove the dust cap and any locking ring from the valve. Push the valve inside the tyre and then gently pull the inner tube out.

4. Partially inflate the tyre and pass it close to your ear until you hear a hiss (or close to your cheek or lips to feel the escaping air). Locate the puncture and mark it with a cross, using the crayon you should have in the puncture repair kit. (It is not often that you need to use a bucket of water to locate a puncture: you can almost always hear it or feel it.)

5. Deflate the tyre by pushing in the valve. Hold the tyre so that the section with the puncture is tight over your knuckles. If you have sandpaper in the repair kit, lightly roughen the area around the puncture.

6. Spread the glue thinly over the puncture, covering an area slightly larger than the patch you are going to use. Leave to dry for at least five minutes. This is the stage at which many people go wrong: they try to fix the patch too soon. The glue is not an adhesive, it actually melts the rubber.

*Above:* It's worth learning how to mend a puncture.

7. While waiting for the glue to do its stuff, check the inside of the tyre for any obvious thorn or piece of glass which may have caused the puncture. Run your finger slowly and sensitively around the inside of the tyre to see if you can find the cause of the puncture.

8. After waiting for at least five minutes for the glue, select a patch, remove the foil and push the patch firmly into the middle of the gluey area. Peel off the backing paper. If you have a lump of chalk in the repair kit, dust the area with some grated chalk.

9. Replace the tube inside the tyre, starting by pushing the valve through the hole in the rim. Ensure that the tube is completely inside the tyre, then using only your hands (ie NOT the tyre levers) gently ease the tyre back inside the rim. The last section will be the hardest; use the heel of the palms of your hands and your thumbs to roll the last part back inside the rim.

10. Reinflate the tyre and replace the locking ring and the dust cap. Replace the wheel into the frame of the bike and do the nuts up tightly, ensuring that it is set centrally (check by spinning the wheel and seeing if it rubs against the frame). Reattach the brakes if you have detached the cable.

*Above:* Cycle hire in Pentewan, Cornwall.

Some of the more popular cycling areas now have bike-hire centres, notably at the more popular railway trails and some of the designated Forestry Commission trails. They offer a good opportunity to test different bikes, to give a non-cyclist a chance of trying out cycling, or can save the hassle of loading up and carrying your own bikes to the start of a trail. Wherever cycle-hire centres exist, they are mentioned in the information section of the route descriptions. It is a good idea to ring beforehand to book a ride, particularly on summer weekends and during the school holidays.

*Above:* In the woods of Wareham Forest.

*Left:* Easy family cycling in the Forest of Dean.

Comfort, freedom of movement and protection against the unexpected shower should be the three guiding factors in deciding what to wear when you go cycling. Specialist cycling clothing is by no means essential to enjoy cycling, particularly on the short and easy rides contained in this book.

## HELMET AND HEADGEAR

The issue of wearing helmets often provokes controversy. Let us hope that it forever remains a matter of personal choice. A helmet does not prevent accidents from happening. Nevertheless, most serious injuries to cyclists are head injuries and helmets can reduce impact.

The case for children wearing helmets is much stronger: they are far more likely to cause damage to themselves by losing control and falling over than an adult. It may be difficult at first to avoid the strap 'pinching' when putting a helmet on a child's head. Bribery of some form or other, once the helmet is securely in place, often helps to persuade the child to see the helmet as a good thing.

In cold weather, a woolly hat or a balaclava is the most effective way of keeping warm. Twenty per cent of body heat is lost through the head.

## THE UPPER BODY

It is better to have several thin layers of clothing rather than one thick sweater or coat so that you can make fine adjustments to achieve the most comfortable temperature. Zips or buttons on sleeves and the front of garments also allow you to adjust the temperature.

Try putting your arms right out in front of you – is the clothing tight over your back? If so, you should wear something a bit looser.

If you are intending to cycle regularly when it is cold, it is worth investing in good-quality thermal underwear and synthetic fleece jackets. These help perspiration to dissipate, do not hold water and dry quickly.

A small woollen scarf and gloves (together with the woolly hat mentioned above) take up very little space and enable you to cope with quite a drop in temperature.

## WATERPROOFS

You are far more at risk from exposure on a wet and windy day than a cold, dry day. The biggest danger lies in getting thoroughly soaked when a strong wind is blowing. Unless you are absolutely certain that it will not rain, it is always worth packing something waterproof. A light, showerproof top takes up little space. If you are buying a waterproof top specifically for cycling, buy a bright-coloured jacket with reflective strips so that you are visible when light is poor.

## LEGS

As with the upper body, what you should be looking for is something comfortable which does not restrict your movement. Tight, non-stretch trousers would be the worst thing to wear — uncomfortable at the knees and the hips and full of thick seams that dig in! Baggy tracksuit bottoms tend to get caught in the chain and can hold a lot of water if it rains. The best things to wear are leggings or tracksters that are fairly tight at the ankle. However, if you feel reluctant about looking like a ballet dancer, then a long pair of socks worn over the bottom of your trousers keeps them from getting oily or caught in the chain.

## CYCLING SHORTS

If you are going to do a lot of cycling then cycling shorts should be the first piece of specialist clothing you buy. They give a lot of padding while allowing your legs to move freely.

## FOOTWEAR

Almost any shoe with a reasonably flat sole is appropriate, although you should bear in mind that few of the trails are sealed with tarmac so there may well be puddles or

*Above:* Remember to wrap children up well on windy days.

even mud in some cases after rain. A pair of trainers or old tennis shoes are a good bet.

NB. Take care to ensure that shoe laces are tied and are not dangling where they could get caught in the chain. The same goes for straps on backpacks and straps on panniers, or particularly long scarves!

*Below:* Lazy cycling by the Exe Canal, south of Exeter.

## WHAT TO TAKE
- Hat, scarf, gloves.
- Waterproof.
- Drink (water or squash is better than fizzy drinks).
- Snacks (fruit, dried fruit, nuts, malt loaf, oatbars).
- Tool kit (pump, puncture repair kit, small adjustable spanner, reversible screwdriver, set of Allen keys, tyre levers, chain link extractor, spare inner tube).
- Guidebook and map (map holder).
- Money.
- Camera.
- Lock.
- Lights and reflective belt (if there is the remotest possibility of being out after dusk).

You can either carry the above in a day-pack or in panniers that fit on to a rack at the rear of the bike. Panniers are the best bet as they do not restrict your movement and do not make your back sweaty.

There are three ways of getting to the start of a ride: cycling there from home; catching a train and cycling to your start point; or carrying the bikes on a car. If you drive, there are three ways of transporting the bikes.

## INSIDE THE CAR

With quick-release skewers now fitted on many new bikes (on the saddle and wheels), it is usually easy to take bikes apart quickly and to fit them into the back of most hatchback cars. If you are carrying more than one bike inside the car you should put an old blanket between each bike to protect paintwork and delicate gear mechanisms from damage.

If you would like to carry your bike(s) inside your car and the idea of quick-release skewers appeals to you, these can normally be fitted by your local bike shop.

Bear in mind that the bikes may be wet and/or muddy when you get back to the car so carry sheets or blankets to protect the upholstery of your car.

## ON TOP OF THE CAR

You can buy special roof-racks which fit on top of cars to carry bikes. On some the bikes are carried upside down, others the right way up; on others the right way up with the front wheel removed.

The advantages of this system are that the bikes are kept separate one from another (ie they do not rub against each other), you can get things out of the boot without problem and they do not obscure visibility.

The disadvantages are that you need to be reasonably tall and strong to lift bikes up on to the roof, it adds considerably to fuel consumption and feels somewhat precarious in strong crosswinds.

## ON THE BACK OF THE CAR

This system seems to be the most versatile and popular method. Different racks can fit almost any sort of car with the use of clips, straps and adjustable angles.

*Above:* Check all straps are tight before driving off.

The advantages of this system are that the rack itself folds down to a small space, the rack can be used on a variety of different cars, you do not need to be particularly tall or strong to load bikes on to the rack and fuel consumption is not as badly affected as by bikes on the top.

The disadvantages are that you may well need to buy a separate hang-on number-plate and rear lighting system if the number plate, braking lights and indicators are obscured by the bikes, the bikes are pressed one against the other and may rub off paintwork and you will restrict access to the boot/hatchback.

The de-luxe system fits on to the back of a towbar, has its own lighting system and keeps the bikes separate as they fit into individual grooved rails. You can buy systems which hold two, three or four bikes.

## GENERAL RULES ABOUT CARRYING BIKES

- Remove all pumps, lights, panniers, water bottles and locks from the bikes before loading them on to the racks.
- Lengths of pipe insulation material are useful for protecting the bikes from rubbing against each other. Try to avoid having delicate parts such as gear mechanisms pushed up against the frame or spokes of the adjoining bike.
- Tie all straps with proper knots. Bows are not good enough.
- Use stretch rubber bungees for extra security, particularly to ensure that the bottom of the bikes is attached to the bumper if you are carrying the bikes on the back of the car.
- If the number plate or brake lights and indicators are obscured you are legally obliged to hang a separate number plate and lights from the back of the bikes.
- It is essential to check and double check all the fixings before setting off and to stop and check again during the course of the journey to ensure nothing has slipped or come loose.

- If you are leaving the bikes on the car for any length of time, lock them to each other and to the rack. While on your ride, it is as well to remove the rack and to lock it inside your car.

## BIKES ON TRAINS

The regulations for carrying bikes on trains seem to change each year and vary from one operator to another, one sort of train to another and according to different times of the day and different days of the week. The only advice that can possibly be given that will remain useful is to take nothing for granted and ALWAYS phone before turning up at the station, to find out charges and availability of bike space. Even then you may find that incorrect information is given out; it is always best to go to the station and talk in person to the railway station staff.

Since privatisation, different companies have adopted different approaches to carrying bikes on trains. The first step is to call the central number 08457 484950 and ask if there are any restrictions on bikes on the train which you want to catch, ie how many bikes are allowed on the train, is there a charge and does the space need to be booked in advance?

*Left:* The ultimate mobile office!

*This page:* Train travel in the good old days!

## FROM REDBROOK TO BIGSWEIR IN THE WYE VALLEY
*(Between Monmouth and Chepstow)*

There are long-term plans to create a largely traffic-free route all the way down the Wye Valley from Hereford to Chepstow, using the dismantled railway line where possible. This ride describes one of the most complete of the present sections, running south from the Boat Inn at Redbrook, reached by a very atmospheric old metal footbridge/railway bridge over the river. The ride then runs alongside the river, at the foot of the steep wooded slopes of the lovely Wye Valley. There are plenty of views of the majestic river, now nearing the end of its course from the mountains of Mid-Wales down to the Bristol Channel at Chepstow. At Bigsweir you cross to the other side of the river and follow a broad stone track south. If you are feeling fit and strong you can continue south for a further 2¹/₂ miles along a rough but beautiful bridleway over the riverside meadows down to the Brockweir Inn. At the moment this section is more of a walk than a ride but it may well improve in the course of the next few years.

**Starting Point and Parking:** In the large car parking area next to the car park for the Boat Inn – diagonally opposite the church on the A466 in Redbrook (3 miles south of Monmouth, and just south of the Clearwell/Newland turn). Grid Reference 536100.

**Distance:** 5 miles one way; 10 miles return (or for just the railway path – 2¹/₂ miles one way, 5 miles return).

**Map:** Ordnance Survey Landranger Sheet 162.

**Hills:** None.

**Surface:** Good stone-based tracks; tarmac. The bridleway beyond the turnaround point (across the riverside meadows towards Brockweir) is very rough.

**Roads and Road Crossings:** The first 2¹/₂-mile section is traffic-free. The route then follows a minor road for 1¹/₂ miles to Bigsweir Bridge where care should be taken crossing the bridge (carrying the A466) to the other side of the river. The third part of the ride (1 mile) is also traffic-free along a broad, stone track.

**Refreshments:** At the Boat Inn, Redbrook. You can reach the Brockweir Inn at Brockweir by following the bridleway south

*Above:* Crossing the beautiful River Wye.

near the river but the last 2 miles are more of a walk than a ride.

ROUTE INSTRUCTIONS:
1. Exit the Redbrook car park in the far left-hand corner by the cypress trees. Take the second track to the right to cross the old railway bridge over the River Wye. Bear left at the Boat Inn and shortly left again on to a broad stone track signposted 'Private Road, No Vehicles'.

2. After 2¹/₂ miles, at the barrier at the end of the track you have a choice:

**ROUTE 1**
REDBROOK TO BIGSWEIR

*Top:* The old railway bridge at Redbrook.

*Above:* The majestic Wye on its course down to Chepstow.

(a) for a totally traffic-free route turn around at this point and return to the start. (b) for a longer ride involving a quiet lane and another offroad section alongside the river continue straight ahead along the lane.

3. After 1½ miles, at the T-junction with the main road, cross on to the pavement opposite **(TAKE CARE)** and turn left over the bridge. About 20yd after the end of the bridge turn right on to the broad stone track between stone pillars signposted 'Public Bridleway. The Hudnalls'.

4. Bear right at two forks of tracks. It is best to turn around at the point where the path starts to climb up towards two tall stone pillars. Although this is a rather arbitrary turnaround point, the way beyond here, which runs along the narrower, lower path beneath this climbing track, soon becomes rough and overgrown and crosses pastureland. It is a beautiful stretch to Brockweir (where there is an inn) but at the moment it is a walk rather than a ride. Improvements are planned for the future. Retrace your steps, **TAKING CARE** on the crossing of Bigsweir Bridge.

# 🚲 ROUTE 2

## THE FOREST OF DEAN

Covering 35 square miles of Gloucester-shire, the Forest of Dean lies on an area of higher land between the River Severn and River Wye and provides spectacular views of the borderland of England and Wales. It represents one of the brightest stars in the firmament of recreational cycling in the whole of Southern England.

A combination of enlightened thinking by the Forestry Commission in its largest holding in the Southwest of the country and co-operation with local authorities, the Sports Council and Sustrans has created an integrated recreational cycling network linking towns with woodland over a large area. The flagship route is the 11-mile Family Cycling Trail which follows disused railway lines for much of its course, providing mostly gentle gradients that are ideal for family cycling. There are challenges at all levels in other parts of the forest.

*Main picture:* Excellent, broad, smooth tracks through the forest.

*Inset left:* The bike hire centre is the focal point for cycling.

*Inset right:* You have been warned!

*Above:* The fascinating railway museum in Coleford.

### Starting Points and Parking:

1. The Pedalabikeaway Cycle Centre near Cannop Ponds in the centre of the Forest of Dean. This is located just north of the crossroads of the B4226 and B4234 between Cinderford and Coleford (about 15 miles southwest of Gloucester).

2. The Railway Museum in the main central car park in Coleford. A 5-mile traffic-free spur leads from Coleford to the Family Trail (ie adding 10 miles there and back to link this to the 11-mile loop). Be warned that this is almost all downhill from Coleford to Parkend so almost all uphill on the way back.

3. There are also shorter spurs from Lydbrook and Cinderford enabling you to join up with the Family Trail.

**Distance:** 11-mile circuit from the Pedalabikeaway Cycle Centre. A further 10 miles if you add the there-and-back spur to Coleford from Parkend.

**Map:** Ordnance Survey Landranger Sheet 162 or better still Outdoor Leisure Sheet 14. The Forestry Commission produces a fold-out leaflet called *Cycling in the Forest of*

*Dean.* This is available from: Forest Enterprise, Crown Offices, Bank Street, Coleford, Gloucestershire GL16 8BA. Tel: 01594 833057.

**Hills:** There is a gradual climb up to the northeast corner of the route.

**Surface:** Good-quality stone and gravel track throughout.

**Roads and Road Crossings:** Several B-roads to cross. Care should be taken with children.

**Refreshments:** At the Cycle Centre. Otherwise you will need to use an Ordnance Survey map to find your way to the various pubs located in the villages nearest to the cycle trail. There is an ice cream van near Cannop Ponds at busy times.

**Cycle Hire:** Pedalabikeaway Cycle Centre, Cannop. Tel: 01594 860065.

**Restrictions:** Unlike farmland or open countryside where the cyclist must keep to the bridlepaths and byways, there are hundreds of miles of forest roads to be explored by bike. There are very few restrictions in the Forest of Dean. Cyclists are welcome in the forests except in the designated conservation areas: the Arboretum (fenced), the National Nature Reserve at Ladypark Wood (fenced) and the Nagshead Nature Reserve (look out for the 'No Cycling' signs). There are other conservation areas within the forest and wet, bog areas are particularly important and vulnerable. By keeping to the tracks there need be no conflict between cyclists and wildlife.

ROUTE INSTRUCTIONS:

1. Facing the Pedalabikeaway Cycle Centre, go to the right, past the Cannop Colliery signpost, to join the yellow 'tyre track' bike trail waymarks. Descend, cross

signposted left, bear right to Drybrook. There is a long steady climb up to Drybrook Road station.

3. Shortly after passing Foxes Bridge there is a steep climb then a long descent, steep at the start, then more gentle. Go past Spruce Ride and Central Bridge.

4. Follow signs for Cannop Wharf and Cycle Centre, at one point turning right where 'Mallards Pike' is signposted straight ahead.

5. Descend steeply from Three Brothers to Cannop Wharf. At the T-junction at the bottom turn right for the Cycle Centre (to the left is the route to Coleford). The route runs briefly along a public road near to Cannop Ponds then bears off to the right on a continuation of the traffic-free trail, soon returning to the Cycle Centre.

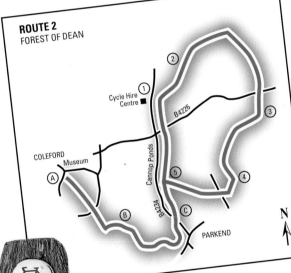

**Spur from Coleford to Parkend and Cannop Wharf**

A. From the central car park in Coleford go past the Co-op supermarket towards the Railway Museum. You will see a bike route signpost with 'Milkwall 1' on it. Cross the road with care and follow the obvious cyclepath now signposted 'Parkend'.

B. After a short climb, descend to cross the road. Continue downhill past the ruins of Darkhill ironworks. At the next road go straight ahead **(TAKE CARE)**.

the road with care on to the path opposite, go up a short steep climb and turn left. Shortly, at a T-junction by a tall wooden signpost, turn left again, signposted 'Drybrook Road Station'.

2. Keep following the yellow tyre track signs in the direction of Drybrook. At a fork, with Lydbrook

C. Continue in the same direction through a rocky cutting following signs for 'Parkend' then 'Cannop Wharf'. The track runs parallel to the road then along Hughes Terrace for a brief lane section. Cross the main road, go past Coleford Junction and on to join the Family Trail at Cannop Wharf. Remember this point if you have started from Coleford and are doing the Family Circuit as well as the Coleford Spur.

## GLOUCESTER & SHARPNESS CANAL

The Gloucester & Sharpness Canal performs the curious function of joining the River Severn to…the River Severn! The tidal rise and fall of the Bristol Channel and the Severn Estuary is one of the highest in the world and makes navigation up the River Severn to Gloucester very tricky. The canal was opened in 1817 and at the time it was the broadest and deepest canal in the world. The towpath is of varying standard: the section which is undoubtedly the jewel in the crown is the 2-mile stretch south of Frampton on Severn which forms part of the National Cycle Network (Route 41, from Gloucester to the old Severn Bridge). Here the surface is excellent. Either side of this section the towpath is more grass and earth: mountain bikes with wide tyres to absorb the bumps are highly recommended. There are long-term plans to improve the quality of the whole towpath.

*Right:* The best stretch of the towpath, south of Frampton.

*Below:* Wonderful stone tower overlooking the estuary.

## ROUTE 3
### GLOUCESTER & SHARPNESS CANAL

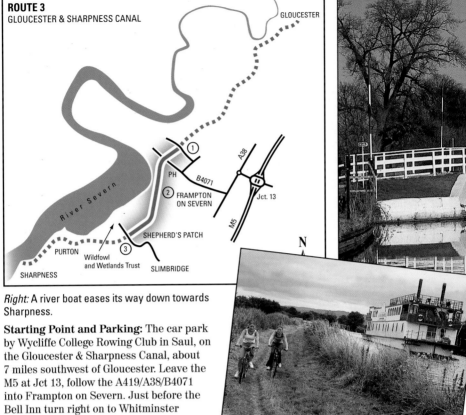

*Right:* A river boat eases its way down towards Sharpness.

**Starting Point and Parking:** The car park by Wycliffe College Rowing Club in Saul, on the Gloucester & Sharpness Canal, about 7 miles southwest of Gloucester. Leave the M5 at Jct 13, follow the A419/A38/B4071 into Frampton on Severn. Just before the Bell Inn turn right on to Whitminster Lane, signposted 'Whitminster'. At the end of the houses turn left, signposted 'Bike Route 41' then, immediately after crossing the canal, turn right. Park in the large car park by the Rowing Club.

**Distance:** It is 15 miles from Sharpness to Hempsted Bridge near to Gloucester. The starting point described here is halfway along the canal, ie it is approximately 7 miles to either end of the canal from here.

**Map:** Ordnance Survey Landranger Sheet 162.

**Hills:** None.

**Surface:** Variable. Stone-based towpath, covered in grass. The 2-mile section south of Frampton is a fine, smooth, gravel path.

**Roads and Road Crossings:** No dangerous crossings.

**Refreshments:** The Bell Inn or the Three Horseshoes PH in Frampton on Severn. Tudor Arms PH at Shepherd's Patch.

ROUTE INSTRUCTIONS:
From the car park by Wycliffe College Rowing Club you have a choice:
A. **To the northeast** you can follow the towpath for 7 miles towards Hempsted Bridge and Gloucester, although there are several rough sections on this stretch. There are plans to improve much of this over the next few years, as funds become available.

*Above:* Still canal days near Frampton on Severn.

B. **To the southwest** you can follow the towpath for 8 miles past Frampton on Severn to Purton and Sharpness. The best section is described below.

### Southwest from Wycliffe College Rowing Club to Patch Bridge.
1. Follow the tarmac lane alongside the canal (with the water to your left). Cross the road at Sandfield Bridge on to the towpath straight ahead. The track is good as far as Fretherne Bridge then soon becomes grassy for less than a mile.

2. At Splatt Bridge (at the southern end of Frampton on Severn) the quality of the towpath improves dramatically: the next 2 miles (as far as Patch Bridge) form part of the National Cycle Network.

3. At Patch Bridge you may wish to return as the track becomes grassy once again as it heads west to Sharpness. The Tudor Arms PH is located on the other side of the bridge. You have three other options:

A. Continue along the towpath through Purton as far as the marina in Sharpness (the most interesting section is the 2-mile stretch from Purton to Sharpness with wide views of the Severn Estuary – this could be done as a separate ride).

B. Return to the start by following the quiet road through the attractive village of Frampton on Severn past the old brick and timber houses, the village ponds and the wide expanse of the village green. To do this, leave the canal towpath at Splatt Bridge.

C. Visit Slimbridge Wildfowl and Wetlands Trust.

## NAILSWORTH TO STROUD RAILWAY PATH
*(10 miles south of Gloucester)*

This attractive, largely wooded ride follows a disused railway along the bottom of the Stroud Valleys, passing close to many of the settlements that grew up in the late Middle Ages as the valleys became the centre of a flourishing cloth trade. Although the path extends further west, from Dudbridge to Stonehouse, it runs at this stage alongside the busy and noisy new bypass and can hardly be deemed a recreational route. By contrast the course of the route from Nailsworth west to Dudbridge appears to be one of those secret hidden passages tucked between the edge of the built-up areas and the surrounding countryside.

HISTORY OF THE RAILWAY
The Stonehouse to Nailsworth branch line was built between 1864 and 1867. A series of financial setbacks led to bankruptcy and the Stonehouse & Nailsworth Railway company was put into the hands of the official receiver late in 1867, just 10 months after opening. The Midland Railway took over and built a separate spur to Stroud, which opened in 1886. The last passenger train ran in 1947 and the branch line was closed in 1966.

*Below:* The railway path uses gentle valley gradients.

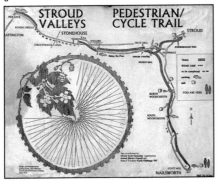

**Starting Points and Parking:**
1. Egypt Mill, Nailsworth. From the roundabout by the clock tower in the centre of Nailsworth take Bridge Street (the A46) towards Stroud and Woodchester. After a short distance, turn first right, signposted 'Egypt Mill' then immediately turn left and park at the far end of the car park at the start of the trail.

2. The Bell Hotel in the centre of Stroud, near the railway station and the roundabout at the junction of the A46 and the A419. Once on your bike, go downhill from The Bell through the subway then uphill past Kwik Fit and the Vet Hospital, following cycle signs for Woodchester.

**Distance:** 5 miles one way; 10 miles return.

**Map:** Ordnance Survey Landranger Sheet 162.

**Hills:** There is a short climb at the Stroud end of the path, from the town centre up to the start of the railway path. There is also one set of steps to negotiate south of Stroud (there is a wheeling ramp alongside the steps).

**Surface:** Good, stone-based track throughout.

**Roads and Road Crossings:** Several minor roads to cross. The A46 is crossed at Rodborough via a traffic island.

**Refreshments:** Lots of choice in Stroud and Nailsworth. The Egypt Mill at the Nailsworth end of the ride serves coffees, lunches and teas.

ROUTE INSTRUCTIONS:
1. From the far end of the Egypt Mill car park in the centre of

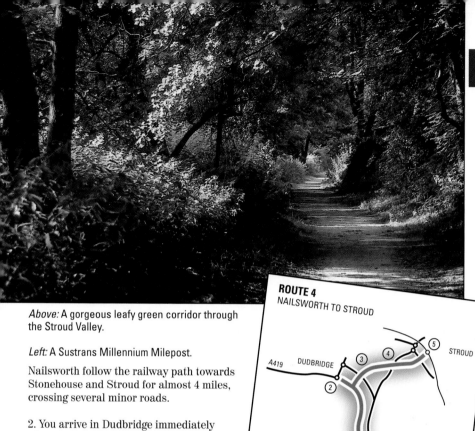

*Above:* A gorgeous leafy green corridor through the Stroud Valley.

*Left:* A Sustrans Millennium Milepost.

Nailsworth follow the railway path towards Stonehouse and Stroud for almost 4 miles, crossing several minor roads.

2. You arrive in Dudbridge immediately after passing through a round concrete tunnel about 20yd long. At this point you have a choice:

A. Turn around and return to Nailsworth.

B. Go into Stroud.

3. (To Stroud.) Come back through the tunnel and at the Millennium Milepost turn left downhill through the housing estate, crossing a bridge over a stream. Continue in the same direction, cross the A46 using the traffic island and climb the steps opposite (use the wheeling ramp).

4. Follow the railway path to its end (just after passing beneath the third bridge), where it turns sharp left uphill. At the T-junction with the road, turn right downhill on the shared-use pavement past the Vet Hospital and Kwik Fit.

5. Aim for the subway. At the mini-roundabout by the Bell Hotel go straight ahead beneath the railway bridge to emerge in the pedestrianised centre of Stroud. Retrace your steps.

## ROUTE 5

### COTSWOLD WATER PARK

This route has been created largely by the wardens at the Cotswold Water Park who have done an excellent job managing an ever-changing asset (new gravel pits are constantly being excavated and the course of rights of way diverted.) The well-signposted route takes you among some of the many lakes formed by gravel extraction and along the course of a dismantled railway. Certain sections will be muddy from late autumn to spring and after prolonged rain. If you explore the village of South Cerney in search of refreshments, keep an eye out for a street called 'Bow-Wow'!

**The Railway Path**

The disused railway line used to be the Midland & South Western Junction Railway route between Southampton and Cheltenham. Apart from carrying passengers the line was used to transport hay and milk from the farms of the Upper Thames and was intensively used during the two World Wars when it provided an important link from the Midlands to the South Coast. The track was dismantled in 1965 and was subsequently purchased by Gloucestershire County Council and converted to a public bridleway.

BOW-WOW

Lakes are created after the end of gravel extraction.

**Starting Point and Parking:** South of South Cerney on the B4696 (called the 'Spine Road East') in Clayhill car park/ picnic site, about 4 miles south of Cirencester. The car park is about 2¹⁄₂ miles southwest of the junction of the B4696 with the A419 on the way towards Ashton Keynes (Grid Reference 052953).

**Distance:** 7-mile circuit.

**Map:** Ordnance Survey Landranger Sheet 163. A brochure with a fold-out map called Cotswold Water Park Leisure Guide shows all the footpaths and bridleways in the Water Park. It can be obtained by sending an SAE to Park Office, Keynes Country Park, Spratsgate Lane, Shorncote, Cirencester, Glos GL7 6DF. Tel: 01285 861459. Website: www.waterpark.org. E-mail: info@waterpark.org.

**Hills:** None.

**Surface:** Mainly stone-based tracks with some narrow and rougher sections. Mountain bikes are recommended. The ride is best done in the summer months as some stretches get muddy in winter or after prolonged rain.

**Roads and Road Crossings:** There is a 1-mile section on road through South Cerney (this takes you to the pubs in the village).

**Refreshments:** Royal Oak PH, Eliot Arms PH, Old George Inn in South Cerney.

**Cycle Hire:** Go By Cycle, Lake 32 (Water Park Office), Keynes Country Park, Spratsgate Lane, Shorncote, Cirencester, Glos GL7 6DF. Tel: 07970 419208 (mobile). Website: www.ukwatersports.co.uk.

ROUTE INSTRUCTIONS:
1. From the southeast corner of the Clayhill car park and picnic site (off the B4696/Spine Road East) follow signs for 'Bridlepath Circuit. South Cerney, Cricklade'. (This is the corner furthest from the entrance to the car park.) Cross the motorcycle barrier (made of railway sleepers) and follow the blue arrows to the right on the narrow, stone-based track around the edge of the field.

2. At the end of the first field turn right (blue arrow) along the edge of a second field. Cross a concrete track, turn right then left to continue in the same direction on the bridleway to Waterhay. Go past a lake on the right. At the road go straight ahead, again signposted 'Waterhay'.

3. Cross a major track used by gravel-extraction vehicles. After passing several 'Treacherous Quicksand' signs to the left take the next track to the left (between wire fences) signposted 'Thames Path. Bridleway'.

4. Follow this path for about 2 miles between several lakes. At a T-junction (immediately after a 'railway sleeper' box/barrier) turn left, signposted 'Public Bridleway. South Cerney'. At the next T-junction turn left again (same sign) then shortly after some outbuildings to the right, take the next track right. At the railway path turn left.

5. Go underneath a red-brick bridge then at the crossroads with the busy Spine Road (by a red-brick railway viaduct) go straight ahead. **(TAKE CARE.)**

6. The track runs parallel with the road then where it joins the road (at the start of the houses) turn left to go through South Cerney.* After ³/₄ mile turn left on to Broadway Lane (the Royal Oak PH lies just beyond this turn).

\* To visit the Eliot Arms PH or the Old George Inn (and the street called 'Bow-Wow'!) after about ¹/₂ mile through the village turn right on to Clarks Hay.

7. **(Easy to miss.)** At the end of the houses on Broadway Lane, shortly after passing a road to the right called 'The Leaze', turn right by a wooden 'Public Bridleway' signpost on to a narrow track. Immediately after crossing a small stream turn left on to a narrow gravel path. This runs between hedges then along a field edge and becomes a broad stone track.

8. Follow the track alongside the lake as it swings round first to the right, then left then right again. Keep an eye out for an easily-missed small path to the left, accessed by a 'V'-shaped stile. (There are plans to remove the stiles at either end of this path to make it more cycle-friendly.) Follow the path to the Spine Road and turn right then left **(TAKE CARE)** to return to the Clayhill picnic site.

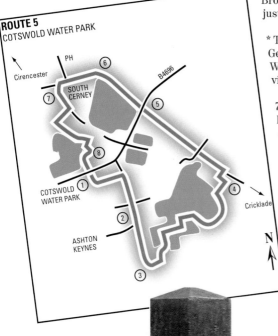

**ROUTE 5**
COTSWOLD WATER PARK

Cirencester
PH
B4696
SOUTH CERNEY
6
7
5
8
COTSWOLD WATER PARK 1
4
Cricklade
2
ASHTON KEYNES
N
3

*Left:* The mighty railway viaduct in the heart of the Water Park.

# THE OLD SEVERN BRIDGE
*(The M48 between Chepstow and Aust)*

It may seem a little bizarre to include in a book about recreational cycling a ride that runs alongside a motorway, but this is no ordinary stretch of wall-to-wall juggernauts. The first Severn Bridge, opened in 1967, has seen its traffic flows slashed with the opening of the Second Severn Crossing, a few miles further south. As a result, as you cycle high above the swirling brown waters of the River Severn, you are more aware of a sense of space and height than noise and traffic fumes. There is a cycleway on both the north and south sides of the bridge. At the Chepstow end these are connected via a conveniently located subway. At the Gloucestershire end it is a bit more complicated! This is a ride best undertaken on a bright sunny day when the wind is not too strong: what may be a gentle breeze elsewhere can be funnelled by the shape of the Severn Estuary into a strong and gusty crosswind.

**Starting Point and Parking:**
1. (English side.) Follow the M4/M48 towards Chepstow. At Junction 1, just before the old Severn Bridge, turn left on the A403 towards Avonmouth then first right towards 'St Augustine's Vineyard, Severn Bridge Maintenance Department'. Park along this minor road.

2. (Welsh side.) From the roundabout at the junction of the A466 and the A48 (on the western edge of Chepstow) take the unsigned minor road running southeast parallel with the A466. At the offset crossroads turn right then left. Park along this road. You can join the cyclepath alongside the A466 which links to the Severn Bridge.

**Distance:** 3 miles one way; 6 miles return.

**Map:** Ordnance Survey Landranger Sheet 162.

**Hills:** There is a noticeable climb up to the centre of the bridge.

**Surface:** Tarmac.

*Below:* Fine views south to the new Severn Bridge.

then some playing fields, the River Wye and the railway line.

3. Follow the track downhill away from the motorway. At the T-junction turn right through the subway under the M48, signposted 'Caldicot, Usk' then at the end of the tunnel turn left uphill and sharp left at the top to recross the bridge on the cyclepath along the north side.
(**OR** *for Chepstow, follow the '4' signs*)

4. Climb to the highpoint of the bridge on the north side, descend to the roundabout by Aust Services. Turn sharp left uphill (use the pavement/concrete track parallel to the road).

5. Go past the petrol station then turn left down the steps that lead to the bridge running across the top of the toll booths, signposted 'Aust, Chepstow'. At the other side of the bridge turn left, signposted 'Aust' then shortly at the T-junction turn right to return to the start.

*Above:* The wonderful, airy cyclepath over the old Severn Bridge.

**Roads and Road Crossings:**
None.

**Refreshments:**
At Aust Services.

ROUTE INSTRUCTIONS:
1. (From Aust.) Climb the minor road that leads towards Old Passage and take the first right, signposted 'No entry except access. Bridge Maintenance Unit'. After 200yd take the first left, signposted 'National Cycle Network Route 4'.

2. Join the cyclepath on the bridge itself. Climb up to the highpoint then go downhill the other side, high above the River Severn

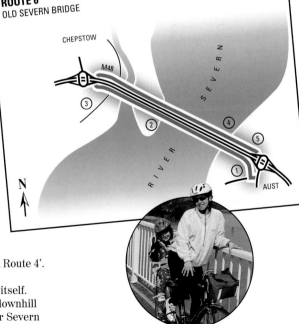

**ROUTE 6**
OLD SEVERN BRIDGE

CHEPSTOW

M48

SEVERN

RIVER

AUST

N

## BRISTOL TO PILL BENEATH THE CLIFTON SUSPENSION BRIDGE

Starting close to the centre of Bristol, this path takes you alongside the River Avon, the tidal river that runs parallel with the Floating Harbour and docks, crossing to the far side of the river via a disused railway bridge then running along the Avon Gorge beneath the famous Clifton Suspension Bridge. When the tidal River Avon is at its lowest, looking more like a stream than a river, it is hard to believe that until the late 18th century Bristol was England's busiest port after London. The path emerges from Leigh Woods, with more open views of the river, and ends at Pill. If you wish to start from Clifton Suspension Bridge you can use a route through Leigh Woods to descend to the gorge.

CLIFTON SUSPENSION BRIDGE
Spanning the Avon Gorge, the bridge is 245ft above high water and has a total span of 702ft. Work started on the bridge in 1836, based upon one of the designs of Isambard Kingdom Brunel, but the bridge was not officially opened until 8 December 1864, some five years after the death of the 'Great Engineer'. Today it is still Bristol's most distinctive landmark. Pilots have flown aircraft beneath the span; suicides and daredevils have jumped from it. The most famous story concerning the bridge is that of Sarah Ann Henley who in 1885 jumped off after a lovers' quarrel but was gently parachuted by her petticoats to the mud below – she lived to be 85.

*This page:* The riverside path beneath the Clifton Suspension Bridge.

*Above left:* Clifton Suspension Bridge.

*Left:* Bristol Cathedral and College Green. *South West Tourism*

**ROUTE 7**
BRISTOL TO PILL

## Starting Points and Parking:

1. From the city centre. The riverside path starts from opposite house number 78 on Cumberland Road. (There is parking just beyond here on the left-hand side of the road, heading away from the centre.) To get here by bike from the Arnolfini Art Gallery cross Prince Street Bridge past the Lifeboat Museum. At the roundabout turn right on to the Cumberland Road, signposted 'CREATE Centre'. Join the pavement cyclepath then 300yd past the footbridge over the river bear left on to the cobbled path by the metal railings opposite house No 78. (You can also join the path from the CREATE Centre itself.)

2. From the Clifton Suspension Bridge. Cross the Suspension Bridge away from Clifton then take the first right on to North Road. Follow this for ³/₄ mile. Just after the third turning on the left you will see the wooden gates on your right into Leigh

Woods (at the top of Nightingale Valley) marking the start of the waymarked cycle track (blue arrows) which eventually drops down through the woods to join the Avon Gorge path. There is parking for several cars near here.

**Distance:** 5 miles one way; 10 miles return.

**Map:** Ordnance Survey Landranger Sheet 172.

**Hills:** The route from the centre of Bristol to the Pill end of the cyclepath is flat. If you start from the Suspension Bridge there will be a climb back up through Leigh Woods on your return. There is also a hill at the Pill end of the ride if you choose to go on beyond the end of the cyclepath to visit the pubs there.

**Surface:** Stone-based track, broad at the Bristol end and becoming narrower as it approaches Pill.

**Roads and Road Crossings:** None, unless you continue on to visit the pubs in Pill.

**Refreshments:** 1. At the CREATE Centre near the start. 2. There are several pubs in Pill, which will involve a short section on road from beyond the end of the cyclepath.

ROUTE INSTRUCTIONS:
1. **(Bristol City Centre.)** From the start of the riverside path opposite No 78 Cumberland Road, follow the cobbled path (with the river to your left) as far as the tall red-brick warehouse then turn left over the grey steel railway bridge to cross the River Avon. Once over the bridge turn right and follow the asphalt path through the park alongside the river (now to your right) to the start of the towpath.

2. The path from Leigh Woods joins from the left after almost 2 miles (by low metal barriers set in a gap in the stone wall to your left).

3. The path ends at Chapel Pill Farm but it is possible to follow the minor road on past

the pond and up past the new housing estate and cricket ground to access the pubs in Pill. At the T-junction beyond the cricket ground there is a pub nearby to the left and several to the right down the hill in the village itself. Retrace your steps.

**Alternative start from Clifton Suspension Bridge/Leigh Woods (top of Nightingale Valley)**
A. Follow the instructions as per 'Starting Points and Parking' to get to the start of the woodland trail through Leigh Woods. Go through the barrier, signposted 'Cycle Track to Pill via Leigh Woods' and follow the short steep climb up and round to the left.

B. At a T-junction turn right then left, following the blue arrows. At the next T-junction, turn right alongside the wall for 50yd then turn left through the gap in the wall.

C. At the T-junction with the road turn right downhill along the line of copper beeches. Follow in the same direction as the tarmac turns to track and descends through the woods.

D. **(Easy to miss.)** Keep an eye out for a post marked with a blue top. Turn right downhill on to a steeper track to join the towpath alongside the river. Remember this point for the return ride.

*Above left:* Relaxing by the marina at Pill, west of Bristol.

*Below:* The autumn colours are a real delight on the riverside path.

## LEIGH WOODS AND ASHTON COURT, NEAR BRISTOL
*(Just west of Clifton Suspension Bridge)*

This mixture of woodland tracks, parkland tracks and minor roads is one of the best circuits near to Bristol that shows the amazing variety of terrain that lies right on the doorstep of the biggest city in the Southwest. The trail starts in beautiful broadleaf woodland, exits into a landscape of mixed arable and pasture with views across the River Severn to Wales and runs past the dark green waters of Abbots Pool and an ancient apple orchard before climbing to the highpoint in Ashton Court where there are great views over the city of Bristol as far east as the hills above Bath. The ride links three off-road sections via some remarkably quiet lanes, bearing in mind their proximity to Bristol. The ride could easily be linked to Ride 7, the Bristol to Pill Riverside Route.

*Right:* Views over Bristol from the top path in Ashton Court Estate.

*Below:* The SS *Great Britain* now lives in Bristol Docks. *South West Tourism*

*Above:* One of several extraordinary bridges along the trail.

*Bottom left:* Bowood House also has a tremendous adventure playground. *South West Tourism.*

*Below:* An old railway sign harks back to the past.

2. Calne: Follow the A4 from the centre of Calne towards Marlborough. At the roundabout turn right signposted 'Station Road Industrial Estate'. Park anywhere along this road. The trail starts alongside the stream near to the roundabout and soon crosses a narrow bridge. Keep the old Wiltshire & Berkshire Canal to your left and cross it via an old red-brick bridge to join the trail to Chippenham.

**Distance:** 6 miles one way; 12 miles return.

**Map:** Ordnance Survey Landranger Sheet 173. This and several other traffic-free routes in the area are shown on the *Severn & Thames Cycle Route Map* (£5.99), available from Sustrans.

**Hills:** No steep climbs.

**Surface:** Tarmac or good-quality gravel path. Some of the woodland stretches will be muddy in the winter and after prolonged rain.

**Roads and Road Crossings:** There is a short section of an estate road in Chippenham and a ½-mile section of quiet lane halfway along the trail.

**Refreshments:** Lots of choice in both Chippenham and Calne.

ROUTE INSTRUCTIONS:
1. From the far left-hand end of the Olympiad car park (ie the corner furthest away from the entrance to the Olympiad) go downhill on a path signposted 'Authorised Vehicles'. Descend to the river and turn left.

2. Keep the river to your right and the golf course to the left. At a crossroads of paths (with a blue bridge to your right) turn left for 100yd then right, skirting round the edge of the housing estate.

3. Join the housing estate road (Riverside Drive) and turn right, keeping the parkland to your right. Follow the road to the end and climb up the zigzag path on to the railway path. **Remember this point for the return trip.** Turn right to cross the bridge.

4. Follow the railway path for 2 miles. Join the lane for ½ mile (at Pound Farm) then, 300yd after passing Rose Cottage on your left, turn left by a Millennium Milepost through a small parking area to rejoin the railway path.

5. Follow the path to its end, go though an ornate metalwork arch, cross the river and the canal, turn right then keep bearing left to emerge on Patford Street in the centre of Calne (the Lansdowne Strand Hotel is just to your left). Retrace your steps.

## THE RIDGEWAY FROM OVERTON HILL (WEST KENNETT) TO BARBURY CASTLE

*(12 miles south of Swindon)*

The Ridgeway is reputed to be the oldest road in Europe, dating back some 5,000 years. It would have been a useful trading route when the valleys and plains below were thickly wooded and still populated by wolves and bears. The surrounding rolling countryside undulates in soft rounded hills, mainly with a patchwork of arable crops interspersed with copses of deciduous trees. The Ridgeway itself is a broad track whose surface varies from chalk and gravel to earth and grass.

It is best to do the ride (on mountain bikes) in the summer months after several hot, dry days: in the winter the track will become muddy with large puddles. The track climbs gently past fields bordered with poppy, vetch and willowherb up to a plateau around 800ft. Barbury Castle is an Iron Age hillfort and is the suggested turnaround point because there happens to be a café here. However, there is nothing to stop you carrying on much further along the Ridgeway or even devising a circular route using the amazing network of bridleways and byways that criss-cross the area.

**Starting Points and Parking:**

1. The layby on the A4 at the West Kennett/Overton Hill start of the Ridgeway (between Calne and Marlborough). This is easy to sail past, but if you slow down at the brow of the hill between West Kennett and West Overton you should find the layby without too much problem (Grid Reference 119681).

2. The parking area on Hackpen Hill on the minor road between Marlborough and Broad Hinton (Grid Reference 129747).

3. Barbury Castle Country Park, at the end of the minor road to the south of Swindon and Wroughton (Grid Reference 158760).

**Distance:** 7 miles one way; 14 miles return.

**Map:** Ordnance Survey Landranger Sheet 173.

**Hills:** A steady climb of 330ft over 3 miles from the start (on the A4) up to the plateau section along Hackpen Hill. There is a second climb of 120ft up on to Barbury Hill.

**Surface:** Variable! Mountain bikes are essential. At best the Ridgeway is a broad, fairly smooth chalk and gravel track. At worst it is more grass and earth than stone (although sections like this are rare). It is best to ride the path between May and October after a hot, dry spell of a few days. The trail is NOT suitable for young children.

**Roads and Road Crossings:** Take care crossing the A4 at the start. After that there are only minor roads or dead-end roads to cross.

*Below:* The enigmatic stones at Avebury.

**Refreshments:** There is a café at Barbury Castle. Otherwise there are pubs near the start of the route in Avebury or West Overton.

ROUTE INSTRUCTIONS:
1. From the layby on the A4 at Overton Hill cross the road and follow the Ridgeway signposted 'Ivinghoe Beacon'.

2. Climb steadily for 3 miles. The gradient levels out. After a further 2 miles, at a crossroads with a minor road go straight ahead.

3. After $1^1/_2$ miles, after a fast descent to the next road junction, turn right then left up through Barbury Castle. At the end of the earthworks go straight ahead across the next field. The café is about 150yd beyond the start of tarmac and the public conveniences.

## THE TARKA TRAIL FROM BRAUNTON TO BARNSTAPLE

This ride forms part of the longest railway path in the Southwest, running almost 30 miles from Braunton to Petrockstowe. Only the section between Braunton and Barnstaple is described here, as the Tarka Trail west from Barnstaple to Bideford then south to Petrockstowe is covered in the first volume of *Cycling Without Traffic: Southwest*. In its entirety the trail encompasses a range of vistas from the broad flat expanses of the Taw/Torridge estuary to the intimacies of wooded riverbanks. The trail threads its way down the River Torridge, passing the ports of Instow and Bideford, the pretty village of Weare Gifford, Canal Bridge, where Tarka the Otter was born and fought his last battle, and on to Petrockstowe. The section described below links Braunton to the handsome town of Barnstaple with its famous Pannier Market, passing brightly painted boats and yellow RAF Rescue helicopters on its way.

**Starting Points and Parking:**
1. **Braunton.** The trail starts by the police station at the far end of the main car park in the centre of Braunton, signposted 'Museum, Tourist Information Centre, Countryside Centre'. Braunton is on the A361 to the west of Barnstaple.

2. **Barnstaple.** The railway station in Barnstaple is a good place to park but starting here will involve pushing your bike for a short distance on the pavement across the main river bridge as you need to get from the south to the north of the river and there is no segregated cycle lane on the bridge. It is best to use the pavement on the east side of the bridge as there is an underpass which takes you on to the start of the trail.

**Distance:** Braunton to Barnstaple – 6 miles one way; 12 miles return.

*Other sections of the Tarka Trail*
1. Barnstaple to Bideford – 9 miles one way.
2. Bideford to Great Torrington – 9 miles one way.
3. Great Torrington to Petrockstowe – 6 miles one way.

*Below:* Bright floral displays in the heart of Barnstaple.

**Map:** Ordnance Survey Landranger Sheet 180. The *West Country Way Map* produced by Sustrans (£5.99) shows this and several other traffic-free trails in Cornwall, Devon and Somerset including the Camel Trail, the Grand Western Canal, the Bridgwater & Taunton Canal, the Willow Walk (Glastonbury) and the Bristol & Bath Railway Path.

**Hills:** None.

**Surface:** Fine gravel surface throughout.

**Roads and Road Crossings:** The only road which presents any difficulty is the main river bridge in Barnstaple. It is suggested you **walk** on the pavement on the east side of the bridge to join the subway under the bridge.

**Refreshments:** Lots of choice in both Barnstaple and Braunton.

**Cycle Hire:** Barnstaple – Tarka Cycle Hire, Railway Station. Tel: 01271 324202.

ROUTE INSTRUCTIONS:
1. From the main car park by the Tourist Information Centre in Braunton head towards the police station. Leave the car park, following signs for 'The Burrows, Barnstaple'. Briefly join the road past Tarka Cycle Hire then turn right on to Station Close and left on to the cyclepath.

2. Follow the trail for 6 miles into Barnstaple, passing Barnstaple Town station. If you wish to continue along the Tarka Trail towards Instow, Bideford and beyond, follow the signposts, passing beneath the river bridge via a subway and **walking** along the pavement to regain the traffic-free cyclepath at the far end of the railway station car park.

*Above right:* A swan made of willow from the nearby Somerset Levels.

*Right:* The Tarka Trail offers fantastic family cycling.

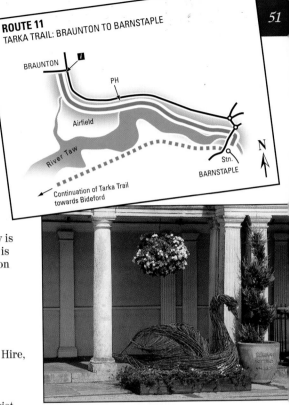

**ROUTE 11**
**TARKA TRAIL: BRAUNTON TO BARNSTAPLE**

BRAUNTON

PH

Airfield

River Taw

Continuation of Tarka Trail towards Bideford

Stn.
BARNSTAPLE

N

## DUNSTER WOODS, EXMOOR
*(4 miles south of Minehead)*

Exmoor is the smallest National Park in
Britain but one which offers a fantastic
amount of top-grade mountain biking as the
area is criss-crossed with byways and
bridleways on well-draining soil. Most of the
mountain biking would be too tough to be
included in the book but there are two
waymarked trails in the forestry to the south
of Dunster which are closer to fitting the bill.
One is described as a Family Route and is a
relatively flat circuit; the other involves a lot
more climbing but is on good, broad stone-
based forest roads which will not deteriorate
in the winter months. This is a good ride to
combine with a trip to Dunster Castle or a
journey on the steam railway that runs
between Minehead and Bishops Lydeard.

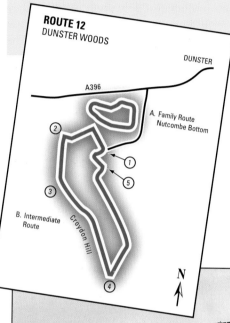

**ROUTE 12**
DUNSTER WOODS

DUNSTER

A396

A. Family Route
Nutcombe Bottom

2

1

5

3

B. Intermediate
Route

Croydon Hill

4

N

**Starting Points and Parking:** From
Dunster take the A396 towards Tiverton.
Less than a mile after the end of the village
(and shortly after crossing a bridge over
the River Avill) take the next lane to the
left. Nutcombe Bottom car park is on the
left, about ³/₄ mile up this steep and narrow
lane. (Grid Reference 978424).

**Distance:** Family Route – 1 mile.
Intermediate Route – 6 miles.

*Below:* Dunster village and castle, north
Exmoor. *South West Tourism*

**Map:** Ordnance Survey Landranger Sheet 181 or Outdoor Leisure Sheet 9.

**Hills:** Lots! There is a relatively gentle one on the Family Route and a much longer one on the Intermediate Route of almost 660ft from the car park to the highpoint on top of Croydon Hill.

**Surface:** Good-quality broad, stone-based forestry roads.

**Roads and Road Crossings:** The minor lane needs to be crossed twice on each route.

**Refreshments:** None on the route. The nearest are in Dunster.

ROUTE INSTRUCTIONS:

A. **Family Route:** Leave Nutcombe Bottom car park, cross the road on to the track opposite and turn right following the green arrows, climbing steadily. **Ignore** the first major track to the left. Continue straight ahead at this point but keep bearing left and keep an eye out for the green arrow pointing you left on to a grassier track. Rejoin the outward route and return to the car park.

B. **Intermediate Route:** The starting point is the upper car park (Grid Reference 974420) about ¾ mile up the hill, on the right, from the Nutcombe Bottom car park. Just as the gradient starts to ease, opposite a 'Dunster Woods Mountain Biking' signpost, turn sharp right on to a broad track into the car park.

*Above:* Broad forestry tracks are ideal for side by side riding.

*Below:* Beautifully handcrafted wooden signposts show the way.

1. Go to the far end of the car park and exit via the far right-hand corner. After a steep descent, go round a sharp left-hand bend at the bottom then start climbing.

2. Climb steadily. At the T-junction with a broad forest road turn right (orange arrow).

3. Keep climbing. Take the **third** broad stone track to the left (orange arrow) to continue uphill. At the crossroads with the tarmac road go straight ahead on to the track opposite; **ignore** tracks to the left and right and keep climbing!

4. Shortly after reaching the brow of the hill and the start of the descent, at an offset crossroads of broad stone tracks, by a four-way wooden waymark turn left downhill, signposted 'Broadwood Farm, Dunster'.

5. Ignore several turns to the right and left on this fast descent with wonderful panoramic views ahead. At the T-junction at the bottom turn left. At the road turn right downhill to return to the car park at the start (take care not to miss this on the fast road descent!).

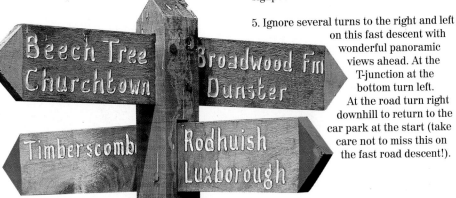

# THE QUANTOCKS RIDGE, WEST OF BRIDGWATER

This is not a cycle trail in the sense of a waymarked forestry route or a railway path. It is a ride on byways and bridleways (where cyclists have a right to ride) along the Quantocks ridge, offering a real 'roof-of-the-world' experience. It is best left for a day of excellent visibility as the views are potentially magnificent, looking north across the expanse of the Bristol Channel to Wales and west towards the hills of Exmoor. It runs along broad stone-based tracks through carpets of heather and gorse at the western end and between avenues of beech trees and high earth banks at the eastern end. If you feel fairly confident with a map it would be possible to put together any number of loops using the ridge as just one part of a spectacular circuit with thrilling descents and steep climbs.

**Warning:** Although the route is along the ridge, there are hills to climb and there will be mud after rain and in the winter, so this ride can be undertaken only on mountain bikes and it is not suitable for young children.

*Main picture:* The views are stupendous on a fine day.

*Inset:* Heather-covered verges line the broad stone tracks.

**ROUTE 14**
WILLOW WALK

WESTHAY

① Visitor Centre

Meare Heath

Shapwick Heath

ASHCOTT CORNER
PH

②

③ ④

GLASTONBURY

⑤

A39

N

*Top:* Glastonbury Tor, seen across the Somerset Levels. *South West Tourism*

*Below:* Chance for refreshment along the Willow Walk.

RAILWAY INN

*Above:* Bridge over the Huntspill River.

*Right:* Rich, dark, peat cuttings seen from the trail.

**Refreshments:** Café in the Craft Shop. The Railway Inn, about halfway along the route. Lots of choice in Glastonbury.

ROUTE INSTRUCTIONS:
1. Leave the Willows Visitor Centre car park and turn left along the lane. **Ignore** the first track to the left. Cross the bridge over the drainage channel and turn immediately left into Shapwick Heath Nature Reserve.

2. After 2 miles, at the crossroads with the minor road go straight ahead (or turn left for 200yd for the Railway Inn).

3. After a further 1½ miles, at a bungalow called 'Sharpham Crossing' by the second road, turn left*. Remember this spot for the return trip – it is 30yd from a post box and telephone box.
*\* Or for a completely traffic-free ride turn around at this point and retrace your steps.*

4. Continue on this lane for a ½-mile to a T-junction. Turn right then immediately left across a black metal bridge to follow a narrow track between planted willow trees.

5. At the next road turn right then at the T-junction with Porchestall Drove turn left. Follow National Cycle Network Route 3 signs past builders' merchants and across a pelican crossing into the centre of Glastonbury. Retrace your steps.

# THE GRAND WESTERN CANAL, TIVERTON

Built 1810-14, the Grand Western Canal was part of a grand coast-to-coast scheme to link Exeter (and the River Exe) to Bridgwater (and the River Parrett), thus enabling ships and their cargoes to avoid the treacherous Cornish coast. The scheme was never fully realised and this is one of the fragments that remain. It runs between Tiverton and Whipcott in mid-Devon. There are two sections of the towpath that are used on the National Cycle Network Route 3 (the West Country Way), connected by 2 miles of quiet lanes through Halberton and Sampford Peverell. The stretch near to Tiverton (described here) is the best-maintained part of the towpath. The canal is used by few boats and is covered in parts by a blanket of water lilies. There are many swans along this section. In the distance there are views of the patchwork of red earth fields and green pastures so characteristic of Devon.

**Starting Point and Parking:** The Grand Western Canal Visitor Centre, Tiverton. From the A361 (North Devon Link Road) follow the A396 towards the centre of Tiverton for 1½ miles. At a sign for 'Police Station, Butterleigh, Grand Western Canal' turn left on to Old Road (leading to Canal Hill). Keep following the brown signs for 'Grand Western Canal'. Start climbing the hill, ignore 'The Avenue' to the left and take the next left signposted 'Grand Western Canal'. Park here and go to the end of the car park to join the towpath.

**Distance:** 3 miles one way; 6 miles return.

**Map:** Ordnance Survey Landranger Sheet 181. The *West Country Way Map* produced by Sustrans (£5.99) shows this and several other traffic-free trails in Cornwall, Devon and Somerset including the Camel Trail, the Tarka Trail, the Bridgwater & Taunton Canal, the Willow Walk (Glastonbury) and the Bristol & Bath Railway Path.

**Hills:** None.

**Surface:** Good gravel surface. Beyond the section described the surface is variable: at best it is a wide gravel-based track; at worst it is a narrow bumpy earth track. There seems to be no logic as to which bits are good quality.

**Roads and Road Crossings:** None, unless you wish to continue along the National Cycle Network Route 3 (the West Country Way) in which case you will need to follow the waymarked route along some quiet lanes through Halberton and Sampford Peverell before rejoining the canal towpath for a further 4 miles to Whipcott.

**Refreshments:** Lots of choice in Tiverton. Tea shop at the start of the ride (at the end of the car park). Pubs in Halberton and Sampford Peverell if you choose to follow the West Country Way (National Cycle Network Route 3).

*Left:* The Grand Western Canal offers flat cycling in hilly Devon!

ROUTE INSTRUCTIONS:
1. Go to the end of the Grand Western Canal car park and bear right up on to the towpath. Follow it for 3 miles, passing beneath Tidcombe Bridge and Warnicombe Bridge.

2. The well-made trail ends at Crown Hill Bridge, made of grey stone. At this point you can return or continue onwards, following the National Cycle Network Route 3 on lanes through Halberton and Sampford Peverell to regain the towpath further east.

*Left:* Water lilies carpet the little-used waterway.

*Bottom:* Tiverton Castle. *South West Tourism*

**ROUTE 15**
GRAND WESTERN CANAL

TIVERTON

HALBERTON

Grand Western Canal

N

## ABBEYFORD WOODS, OKEHAMPTON
*(2 miles north of Okehampton)*

Set on the northern edge of Dartmoor National Park, the attractive town of Okehampton has the potential to become a real centre for recreational cycling: the Devon Coast to Coast Route (part of the National Cycle Network) passes through here; there is a good traffic-free section between Meldon Viaduct and Lake Viaduct (see Route 17) which is being extended in both directions; to the south of Okehampton Camp the Military Loop Road takes you right up into the heart of Dartmoor (see Route 18); there is a fine network of lanes to the north, east and west; and then there are the tracks around Abbeyford Woods, described here. These are good, broad, stone-based forest roads, ideal for 'conversational' cycling as you can ride two abreast without worrying about traffic.

**Abbeyford Woods**
The fertile brown soil is ideal for the Douglas fir and larch trees that produce high-quality logs for construction. The younger thinnings are removed to provide pulp for newsprint. The gales of early 1990 brought down hundreds of trees in the forest. These have now been replanted to provide timber in the future. The old oak and beech trees are now managed for landscape and conservation.

**Starting Point and Parking:** The car park in the middle of Abbeyford Woods on the minor road to the north of Okehampton that runs from the B3217 (Exbourne Road) towards Jacobstowe (Grid Reference 589975).

**Distance:** 4-mile circuit.

**Map:** Ordnance Survey Landranger Sheet 191.

**Hills:** There are two main climbs, one in the middle of the ride (the longer of the two) and one at the end.

**Surface:** Broad, stone-based forest roads.

**Roads and Road Crossings:** There is a short section of minor lane used at the beginning of the ride. This is mainly downhill, so you won't spend long on it. The same minor road is crossed twice in the second half of the route.

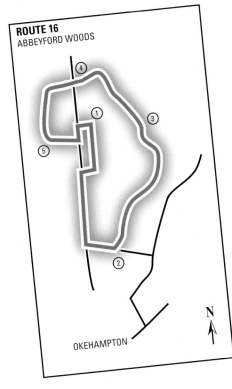

**Refreshments:** None on the route. The nearest are in Okehampton.

ROUTE INSTRUCTIONS:
1. From the car park follow the track that starts by the wooden barrier near to a 'Horse' sign. At the T-junction at the end of this section turn right then at the road turn left.

2. **(Easy to miss!)** Go down a steep hill and shortly after the end of the **second** sharp left-hand bend turn left into the car parking area towards a wooden barrier.

*Above:* Cyclists share the tracks through the woods with horseriders.

*Opposite:* Okehampton Castle. *South West Tourism*

3. Go down then up, following this track around several sharp bends. At the T-junction with a major forest road turn right (there is a 'Tarka Trail' wooden post straight ahead).

4. Follow the edge of the woodland with fine views out across the Okement Valley. At the T-junction with the road turn left then after 100yd turn right on to a narrower track by wooden barriers.

5. Descend. At the T-junction with a major forest road turn left. Follow this major trail around a sharp left-hand bend uphill. At the crossroads with the minor lane go straight ahead on to a track between wooden barriers and bear left to return to the car park.

## MELDON VIADUCT TO LAKE VIADUCT, DARTMOOR
*(South of Okehampton)*

As one of the most progressive local authorities in the country with regard to recreational cycling, Devon is creating many new cycle routes: the Devon Coast to Coast Route (part of the National Cycle Network) will within a few years offer a largely traffic-free route all the way from Ilfracombe on the north coast down to Plymouth on the south coast. The ride described here forms part of the middle section, along the course of an old dismantled railway linking the magnificent Meldon Viaduct to Lake Viaduct. There are superb views into the heart of Dartmoor and across to the west over the rolling patchwork of fields and hedgerows so typical of Devon. A steam engine runs between Okehampton station and Meldon Viaduct on the preserved Dartmoor Railway most summer weekends so it would be easy to combine the bike ride with a trip on the wonderfully restored old train. There are plans to extend the route in both directions: parallel with the railway line back to Okehampton and southwest towards Lydford and beyond.

*Overall:* Typical Dartmoor scenery as seen from the railway path.

*Above:* The extraordinary Highwayman Inn at Sourton.

the laybys up this lane are for passing quarry trucks and not for car parking. You have been warned!

**Distance:** 3¹⁄₂ miles one way; 7 miles return.

**Map:** Ordnance Survey Landranger Sheet 191. The *Devon Coast to Coast Map* produced by Sustrans (£5.99) shows this and several other traffic-free trails in Devon including the Ilfracombe Railway Path, the Tarka Trail, the Okehampton Military Loop Road, the Princetown Tramway and the Plym Valley Trail.

**Starting Points and Parking:**
1. **The Meldon Reservoir car park**, southwest of Okehampton (Grid Reference 562918). Follow the B3260 from the centre of Okehampton for 3 miles towards Launceston. Immediately after crossing the bridge over the A30 continue straight ahead on to the no through road. Climb for about ¹⁄₂ mile and turn left immediately after passing beneath the railway bridge. You will need to return to this spot on your bikes. The car park is about ¹⁄₃ mile up this lane.

2. **Sourton Down**. Near the Bottle Neck Inn at the junction of the A386 and A30 to the southwest of Okehampton. Follow the A386 south from the A30 and take the first left, signposted 'Sourton Down'. The access to the railway path lies opposite house No 3, along a narrow track between stone walls.

3. **Sourton**. There is parking for a few cars by the church at Sourton on the lane opposite the Highwayman Inn (A386). Please park with consideration.

4. **Lake.** If you ask at the Bearslake Inn at Lake (A386) they may allow you to park if it is not during a busy period.

5. **Meldon.** This is by far the worst of the options as you are faced with a very steep climb up steps from beneath the viaduct. There is little space for parking nearby and

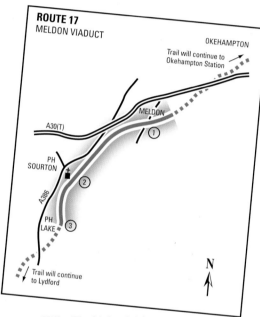

**ROUTE 17**
MELDON VIADUCT

OKEHAMPTON

Trail will continue to Okehampton Station

MELDON

A30(T)

①

PH
SOURTON

②

A386

PH
LAKE ③

Trail will continue to Lydford

N

**Hills:** The highpoint is about halfway along so there is a gentle climb from either end up to this point.

**Surface:** Tarmac or fine gravel path.

**Roads and Road Crossings:** None.

**Refreshments:** The 'Buffet Car' at the station at Meldon Viaduct; the Bottle Neck Inn, Sourton Down (just off the route); the Highwayman Inn, Sourton (just off the route); the Bearslake Inn, Lake (just off the route).

ROUTE INSTRUCTIONS:
1. From the Meldon Reservoir car park go back down to the railway bridge and climb up on to the railway path. Turn **right** for Meldon Viaduct (the path will eventually go all the way to Okehampton railway station) or left for Lake Viaduct (the trail will continue on towards Lydford in the future).

2. You can visit the Highwayman Inn by leaving the path at Sourton church and descending the stone track to the A386. (**Take great care** crossing the road.)

3. You can visit the Bearslake Inn by leaving the path at the end of Lake Viaduct and turning sharp left down on to the tarmac access ramp and left again on the stone track that leads down to the A386.

*Right:* Recalling the delights of rail travel in the steam age.

*Below:* Moorland views from Meldon Viaduct.

*Below right:* The stone viaduct near Meldon.

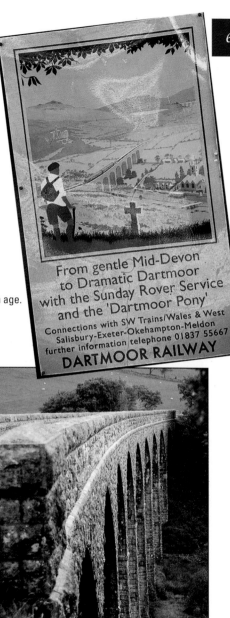

## OKEHAMPTON MILITARY LOOP ROAD

*(2 miles south of Okehampton)*

This ride offers you the chance to climb right into the heart of Dartmoor on a little-used public road that forms a loop, ie it carries no through traffic. The drawbacks are that you have a climb of 550ft and that you will be sharing the route with the odd vehicle. On the plus side are some of the best views from all Dartmoor, a fine sense of achievement when you get to the highest point, and one of the most wonderful descents in the whole book! This is definitely a ride to leave for a day of good visibility as you deserve to be rewarded for all your efforts with the far-ranging panorama that can be enjoyed from the top. If there are several of you who have arrived in the same vehicle, why not persuade the driver to let the rest of you continue downhill on your bikes from the start point all the way into Okehampton, a drop of a further 700ft! If you enjoy this ride there is another (even tougher) climb from Bridestowe up into the heart of the moor (see 'Other Routes in Brief', page 103)

**Warning:** The road is occasionally shut when the ranges are being used for firing. Details of range firing programmes are obtainable from Okehampton Tourist Information Centre (Tel: 01837 53020).

**Starting Point and Parking:** At the fork of roads at Grid Reference 597922, to the south of Okehampton. From the centre of Okehampton follow signs for 'Station' and 'Okehampton Camp'. Follow the road up over the A30 bypass and past Okehampton Camp. Cross the cattle grid, continue straight ahead then at the first major fork of tarmac roads park in the car parking area.

**Distance:** 7-mile loop.

**Map:** Ordnance Survey Landranger Sheet 191 or Outdoor Leisure Sheet 28.

**Hills:** This is a strenuous ride with a climb of 550ft from the start to the highest point. The final mile of the climb is the steepest.

**Surface:** Tarmac or good gravel track throughout.

**Roads and Road Crossings:** The road is open to cars, although there is very little traffic as there are sections where the tarmac is rough or missing and the road goes nowhere anyway!

*Right:* Wild Dartmoor ponies bemused by passing cyclists.

*Far right:* An adventurous ford across the Military Loop road.

**Refreshments:** Lots of choice in Okehampton.

ROUTE INSTRUCTIONS:
1. From the car parking area take the left-hand fork. Descend to cross Black-a-ven Brook then climb steadily.

2. The gradient steepens near to the top of the climb, which you reach when you pass a dry-stone wall shelter/lookout post.

3. Enjoy the fabulous descent back to the start. If there are several of you, try persuading the driver to let the rest of you cycle right down into the centre of Okehampton, another 700ft of descent!

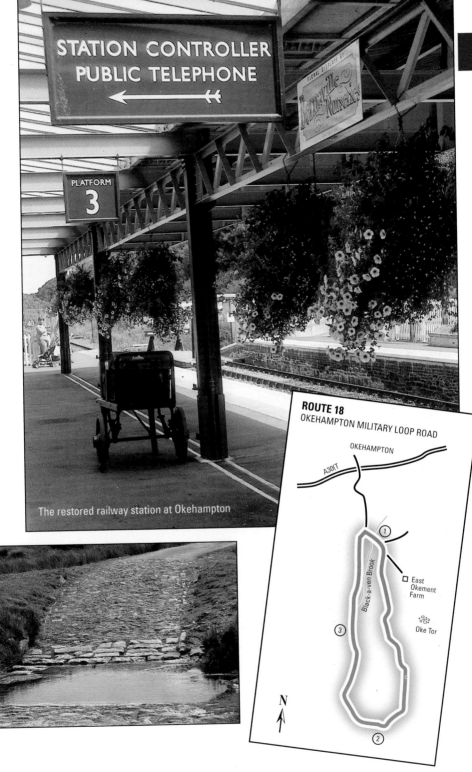

STATION CONTROLLER
PUBLIC TELEPHONE

PLATFORM
3

The restored railway station at Okehampton

**ROUTE 18**
OKEHAMPTON MILITARY LOOP ROAD

OKEHAMPTON

A30/T

East
Okement
Farm

Oke Tor

Black-a-ven Brook

N

## BELLEVER FOREST, DARTMOOR
*(12 miles northeast of Tavistock)*

There are three main Forestry Commission
holdings set close together on high
Dartmoor that can be used for recreational
cycling: Bellever, Soussons Down and
Fernworthy. Of the three, Fernworthy is the
largest but least accessible, Soussons Down
is the smallest and Bellever is between the
two in size but the easiest of access. The
entrance is just off the B3212, the main
road across the moor between Tavistock
and Moretonhampstead. As might be
expected for a ride in such a hilly area
there are a couple of testing climbs, the
second one steep enough to require you to
push your bike for a short distance. This is
not a waymarked forestry ride but as the
woodland is fairly small and the instructions
fairly few you shouldn't get lost. The ride
drops at one point down into the valley
formed by the East Dart, one of several
important Devon rivers that rise on the high
moorland; it joins the West Dart a little
further south and makes its way to the
coast at Dartmouth.

**Surface:** Good stone-based forest roads for most of the ride. One steep, grassy then stony section after the Bellever Youth Hostel.

**Roads and Road Crossings:** None, unless you choose to return on the lane from the Youth Hostel back to the start.

**Refreshments:** None on the route. The closest are in Postbridge.

ROUTE INSTRUCTIONS:
1. From the car park off the B3212 at Postbridge take the furthest left of the three tracks through a wooden barrier on to a steadily climbing track.

**ROUTE 19**
**BELLEVER FOREST**

POSTBRIDGE

Moretonhampstead

B3212

Princetown

Shortcut

N

2. **Ignore** a right turn after 300yd and a left turn after a further 400yd. At a junction of five tracks at the end of a clearing follow the main, broad, winding forestry road to the left.

3. You soon enjoy a fast descent, ignoring two turnings to the left. After a short climb follow the track round to the left for a second fast descent.

4. At the T-junction with picnic tables ahead, turn left. At the road, for a **shortcut** (avoiding a short steep, rough push) go straight ahead, climbing then descending. For the **main route** turn left. At the end of the tarmac continue straight ahead up a steep grassy slope, signposted 'Path'. You will have to walk this section.

5. The steep grassy track turns stony. At the fork at the gate with a 'Lichway' sign on it, bear right and continue steeply uphill. At the crossroads with a broad, stone forest road turn right. Climb, then at the T-junction with another forest road bear right to rejoin the outward route for a fast descent back to the start.

*Left and above:* Views of the forest.

**Starting Point and Parking:** There is a car park at the edge of the forest to the southwest of Postbridge, just off the B3212 (Grid Reference 646787).

**Distance:** 5-mile circuit.

**Map:** Ordnance Survey Landranger Sheet 191.

**Hills:** There are two main climbs – one long steady 200ft climb right from the start then a shorter but steeper and rougher 300ft climb after passing the Youth Hostel in Bellever.

*Overall:* The grey and forbidding bulk of Dartmoor Prison.

## EXE VALLEY AND EXETER CANAL THROUGH EXETER

A long traffic-free route starts in the very heart of Exeter and follows a combination of the River Exe and the Exe Canal down to the wide expanse of the Exe Estuary at Turf Locks. The River Exe and its tributary the River Culm drain much of Exmoor and the Blackdown Hills making Exeter prone to flooding. Weirs and defence works have reduced the risk, creating at times a bewildering amount of water channels and possible paths to follow. All paths lead south to Turf Locks! The section through the city centre passes the attractive marina where brightly coloured dinghies tack and jibe. Further south there is an option of following the river or the canal, the latter passing the popular Double Locks Inn. Beyond the major road bridge the towpath becomes narrower and at times a little overgrown, although the surface is very good by general canal towpath standards.

**Starting Points:** The route can be picked up at several points all the way along the riverside through Exeter. It runs along the west side of the river from near St David's railway station to the canal basin then along the Exeter Canal past the Double Locks Inn to the Turf Inn.

**Parking:** There is a car park on Station Road, just across the river from St David's railway station, off Cowley Bridge Road (the A377 on the northwest side of Exeter).

**Distance:** 9 miles one way; 18 miles return.

**Map:** Ordnance Survey Landranger Sheet 192. Better is the *Exeter Cycle Guide and Map* produced by Exeter City Council. Available from the Tourist Information Centre. Tel: 01392 265700.

**Hills:** None.

**Surface:** Tarmac through the city centre, generally good stone-based track alongside the canal. As you get further away from the city centre the track is at times a bit rougher and more overgrown.

## ROUTE 20
### EXE VALLEY

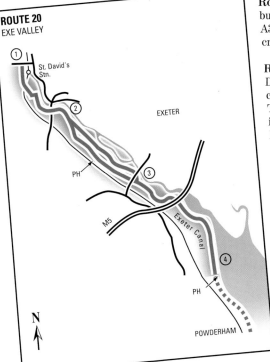

**Roads and Road Crossings:** The only busy road to cross, Bridge Road (the A379 on the south side of the city), is crossed via a pelican crossing.

**Refreshments:** Lots of choice in Exeter; Double Locks Inn, halfway between the city centre and Bridge Road (the A379); Turf Inn, at the end of the canal where it joins the Exe estuary (southeast of Exminster).

ROUTE INSTRUCTIONS:
1. From the car park off Station Road (just over the river from St David's railway station), follow signs for 'Exe Bridges, City Centre'. The route passes beneath a railway bridge then rejoins the river.

2. At the start of the canal you have a choice of following a route through the Riverside Valley Park or alongside the canal. The canal route will take you past the Double Locks Inn.

3. Both routes rejoin at Bridge Road (A379) where there is a pelican crossing to enable you to follow the canal towpath further south.

4. The path narrows and may be overgrown. Please show consideration to other users. Continue on under the M5 bridge to the Turf Inn. Retrace your steps.

*Above left:* Exeter Docks from the cycle trail alongside the Exe.

*Below left:* Exeter Cathedral. *South West Tourism*

*Below:* The popular Double Locks Inn makes a welcome stopping point.

## EXMOUTH TO BUDLEIGH SALTERTON

Starting conveniently from Phear Park in the centre of the seaside town of Exmouth, this ride heads east along the course of a recently improved railway path towards Budleigh Salterton. The trail climbs gradually through woodland then drops down towards Knowle. If you wish to visit the attractive seaside town of Budleigh

Salterton you will need to use a combination of quiet lanes and residential streets to reach the shops, cafés and pubs. If it is a hot summer's day and a swim in the sea beckons, there is an excellent beach at Sandy Bay, to the southeast of Exmouth.

**The Railway Path**
Work on the Budleigh Salterton Railway began in 1899, and the line to Exmouth, completed by the London & South Western Railway, opened in 1903. It ran for over 60 years but was closed during the era of the Beeching cuts in 1967.

*Left:* The beach at Budleigh Salterton.

**Distance:** 4 miles one way; 8 miles return.

**Map:** Ordnance Survey Landranger Sheet 192.

**Hills:** There is a gentle climb of 260ft from the start to the highpoint in the woodland near to Knowle.

**Surface:** Good-quality tarmac or stone path.

**Roads and Road Crossings:** The busiest road on the traffic-free section is crossed via a pelican crossing. If you wish to continue right into the heart of Budleigh Salterton and the seafront you will need to use lanes, residential streets and the main shopping street in the town.

**Refreshments:** There is a café in Phear Park in Exmouth. The traffic-free route does not pass any refreshment stops but there is plenty of choice in Budleigh Salterton beyond the end of the railway path.

**Starting Point and Parking:** The free car park in Phear Park to the northeast of the centre of Exmouth. If approaching from the north on the A376 you should turn left off the Exeter Road on to Gipsy Lane before reaching the town centre. Gipsy Lane comes shortly after Hulham Road (also on the left).

ROUTE INSTRUCTIONS:
1. Leave the free car park in Phear Park, return past the café, go over the bumps and exit the park through the opening with bollards and eagle-topped stone pillars. Turn left on the pavement up Marlpool Hill and shortly afterwards take the first left, signposted 'Littleham Cycle Route'.

*Right:* Buddleia in full bloom along the railway path.

2. The route follows first a flat section then a short climb to the road. Bear right on to the shared-use pavement. Cross the main road (B3178) using the pelican crossing and turn left, following signs for Budleigh Salterton. At the end of the alley go straight ahead on to the green-painted cyclepath (Jarvis Close).

3. Follow cycle signs to cross a wide road via a traffic island, turn right along the pavement then shortly afterwards turn left, following signs for Budleigh Salterton. Follow the trail out into the countryside, climbing gently through lovely broadleaf woodland.

4. Shortly after passing the Millennium Milepost the trail turns right, climbs and ends at a T-junction with a minor lane. If you do not want to go on roads and prefer to stay on the traffic-free path then turn around at this point and retrace your route.

**5. (On to Budleigh Salterton by road.)** At the T-junction with the minor lane (Bear Lane), at the end of the traffic-free trail, turn right then at the next T-junction (with the busier B3178) turn left then right on to Bedlands Lane. At the T-junction at the end of Bedlands Lane turn right and follow the road around to the left.

6. At the T-junction at the end of Moor Lane turn right and follow this downhill into the centre of Budleigh Salterton. If you wish to visit the beach turn left at the traffic lights along the High Street for ¹/₄ mile. From wherever you choose to finish the outward ride, retrace your steps back to Exmouth via Station Road–Moor Lane–Bedlands Lane–Bear Lane–cyclepath–Phear Park.

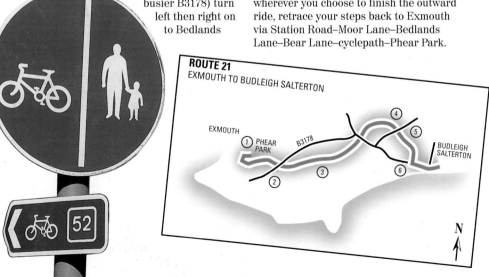

**ROUTE 21**
EXMOUTH TO BUDLEIGH SALTERTON

EXMOUTH

① PHEAR PARK   B3178

②   ③   ④   ⑤   ⑥

BUDLEIGH SALTERTON

N

52

Fishing boats beached on the shingle at
Budleigh Salterton

## CARDINHAM WOODS
*(2 miles east of Bodmin)*

There are few Forestry Commission holdings of any real size in Cornwall. With the exception of Idless Woods to the north of Truro (see 'Other Routes in Brief' on page 103) there is only a scattering of smallholdings along the A389 and A38 between Wadebridge, Bodmin and Liskeard. Of these, Cardinham Woods is the largest and it is possible to devise several short rides within the woodland, of which this is just one.

**Cardinham Woods**

The Forestry Commission bought Cardinham Woods in 1922. Today their fertile soils produce fine timber, saw logs for house building from the impressive old Douglas firs, and pulp for newsprint from the younger thinnings. Nearly 80 years of careful management has created a varied and attractive forest. Each age of tree is home to a different range of wildlife. Look out for ravens and buzzards soaring above the forest. You may catch the occasional glimpse of grey squirrels, rabbits or foxes. Red and roe deer are here but melt away into the forest at the first hint of danger.

*This page:* Bodmin Gaol. *South West Tourism*

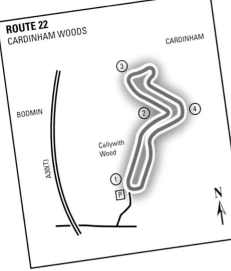

**ROUTE 22**
**CARDINHAM WOODS**

CARDINHAM

BODMIN

A30(T)

Callywith
Wood

3

2

4

1

P

N

ROUTE INSTRUCTIONS:

1. Go to the end of the car park, cross the stone bridge and turn right by a black and white wooden barrier by a signpost marked 'All walks begin here'. Take the right-hand of the three tracks, signposted 'All ability route. Ladyvale Bridge'.

2. Climb steadily. At the T-junction turn left, signposted 'Lidcutt Valley 2kms'.

3. At the next major junction of tracks, at the bottom of a short descent, turn right, again signposted 'Lidcutt Valley' and cross a small stream.

4. At the bottom of a fast descent take the second track on the right, ie cross a **second** bridge over the stream with low wooden barriers either side of the bridge. Shortly afterwards turn right again, signposted 'Car park'. Go round a black and white barrier to join a tarmac lane and return to the car park.

**Starting Point and Parking:** The car park in Cardinham Woods at Grid Reference 100666. From Bodmin take the A38 towards Liskeard for 2 miles. Cross the bridge over the A30 dual carriageway then after ¼ mile turn left along a road signposted 'Cardinham, Fletchersbridge'. Shortly after a sharp right-hand bend, turn left and follow signs for the Cardinham Woods car park.

**Distance:** 3-mile circuit (with plenty of opportunities to extend and explore further).

**Map:** Ordnance Survey Landranger Sheet 200.

**Hills:** Long gentle climb at the start of the ride.

**Surface:** Broad, stone-based forest road.

**Roads and Road Crossings:** A minor no through road is used at the end of the ride.

**Refreshments:** None on the route. The nearest are in Bodmin.

*Above right:* Father and son enjoy the delights of Cardinham.

*Right:* One of the few signposts in the woods.

LIDCUTT VALLEY

Footpath to Racecourse Downs

## PORTREATH TO DEVORAN, COAST TO COAST ACROSS CORNWALL

*(4 miles north of Camborne)*

The Mineral Tramway route from the north coast of Cornwall at Portreath to Devoran in the south is destined to become Cornwall's second most popular cycle trail after the Camel Trail. The result of many years of patient negotiation and engineering, the trail uses several sections of old tramroad that used to serve the mines that are scattered around this part of Cornwall. Many of the old ruins and chimneys are still visible. The route climbs gradually from the attractive seaside resort of Portreath through Cambrose to Wheal Rose and Scorrier. From this highpoint the trail drops down into the Poldice Valley and along the Carnon River down to Devoran, passing beneath the soaring railway viaduct. The route is generally well waymarked with handsome granite stones but there are a couple of places (particularly in Scorrier) where you should keep a sharp eye out for signposts.

**Starting Points and Parking:**
1. The car park by the beach in Portreath, on the B3300 to the north of Camborne/Redruth.
2. The car park by Bissoe Cycle Hire Centre, about 5 miles southwest of Truro (Grid Reference 772415).
3. The car park by the village hall on Quay Road in Devoran, just south of the A39 between Truro and Falmouth (Grid Reference 792393).

**Distance:** 11 miles one way; 22 miles return.

**Map:** Ordnance Survey Landranger Sheets 203 and 204 or Explorer 104.

**Hills:** Gradual 330ft climb from Portreath or Devoran up to Scorrier in the middle of the ride.

**Surface:** Generally good quality with the occasional rougher patch.

**Roads and Road Crossings:** Several minor road crossings and several short sections of road (mainly quiet) are used.

*Below:* The dramatic North Cornwall Coast at Portreath.

*Right:* A typical Cornish engine house, now in ruins.

There is a busier road section through Scorrier where care should be taken. If you decide to visit the pub in Devoran the A39 is extremely busy and should be crossed with **GREAT CARE**. (There are plans to improve this crossing.)

**Refreshments:** Lots of choice in Portreath; Plume of Feathers PH, Fox & Hounds PH, Scorrier; Old Quay Inn, Devoran.

ROUTE INSTRUCTIONS FROM PORTREATH TO DEVORAN (NORTH TO SOUTH):
1. Leave the car park by the beach in Portreath and follow the B3300 towards Redruth. At the Portreath Arms bear left on to Sunnyvale Road signposted 'Portreath Tramroad'.

2. After ½ mile, just before rejoining the B3300, bear left uphill on to the start of the traffic-free trail. Continue in the same direction on a generally level track at several minor junctions.

3. After 2 miles, briefly join a minor road, continuing in the same direction. At the T-junction turn right then cross the more

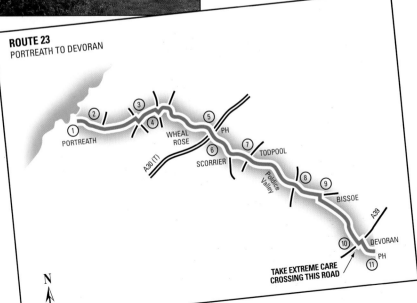

**ROUTE 23**
PORTREATH TO DEVORAN

PORTREATH

WHEAL ROSE

A30 (T)

SCORRIER

PH

TODPOOL

Poldice Valley

BISSOE

A39

DEVORAN

PH

TAKE EXTREME CARE CROSSING THIS ROAD

N

*Left:* A new section of path runs past the old spoil heaps.

8. Stay on the upper, right-hand track down the valley. After 1½ miles the track turns to tarmac. Join a road by a stone barn and continue straight ahead, then after 300yd, by a granite signpost, turn left off the road to rejoin the traffic-free route.

9. Follow the main broad stone track in the same direction. Shortly after the tall metal Millennium Milepost turn sharp right downhill, soon turning sharp left to continue dropping height. Go past Bissoe Cycle Hire. At the road turn right then left on to a track.

major road and turn left on to the parallel light brown cycle track, following the granite waymarks.

4. Take the first road to the right. At the crossroads go straight ahead on to a lane, then at the second crossroads go straight ahead on to a broad, gravel track.

5. At the crossroads (with a small model of a Cornish engine house in the garden of the house on your left) turn left and go past a scrapyard. At the second T-junction turn right on to the cyclepath/pavement then at the third T-junction also turn right (following the cyclepath) to cross the bridge over the A30.

6. Using the traffic islands at the crossing point, turn right on to the A3047 signposted 'Redruth' then take the first left to go past the Crossroads Motel. Go under the railway bridge and immediately after the Fox & Hounds PH turn right through the car park. Cross the next road using traffic islands, turn left along the pavement then first right, following granite waymarks.

7. Follow this track downhill, crossing the road on to a continuation of the cyclepath. The track turns to tarmac. At the T-junction bear right. At the crossroads go straight ahead signposted 'Todpool' then as the road swings sharply left uphill, turn right on to a track. After 50yd turn left down the Poldice Valley.

10. Cross two minor roads, pass beneath a tall railway viaduct then cross a third road. At the end of the track, at the T-junction with the very busy A39, you have a choice of returning or of continuing on to the Old Quay Inn in Devoran.

11. (Devoran.) Cross the A39 **WITH EXTREME CARE** by turning left (along the pavement) then right on to Greenbank Road. As the road swings left bear right on to Quay Road for about ½ mile for the Old Quay Inn.

ROUTE INSTRUCTIONS FROM DEVORAN TO PORTREATH (SOUTH TO NORTH):
(The south-north route is not shown on the route map as it is, in effect, the north-south route in reverse)

1. From the car park by the Village Hall in Devoran return to the main road (A39). **WITH EXTREME CARE** cross on to the pavement opposite, turn left to cross the bridge over the river then shortly afterwards turn right through a gate on to the start of the trail. After 200yd turn right (signposted 'Portreath') over a narrow wooden bridge to cross the stream.

2. Go straight ahead at a minor lane. Pass beneath the viaduct. Cross straight over two more minor lanes. At a T-junction with a road shortly after a 'Meccano'-type structure turn right then left to go past Bissoe Cycle Hire.

3. Shortly afterwards, follow the main track as it swings round steeply up to the right then sharply left. At the T-junction with the road turn right then after 300yd as the road swings sharp right continue straight ahead on to a broad track to the left of the stone barn.

4. **Ignore** a left turn to a farm then bear left on the upper track at the next two forks. Continue in the same direction through old mining works (stone circles topped with conical wire pyramids). At the T-junction turn right uphill then left on to the lane.

5. At the crossroads of lanes go straight ahead then after 200yd bear left on to a drive/track. Join a newly built cycle track parallel with the busy B3298. Cross the road on to a continuation of the cyclepath.

6. At the crossroads with the main road at the top of the hill, turn left on the pavement. At the end of this section cross the road at the traffic islands and at the Fox & Hounds PH car park turn left on to the road and go under the railway bridge, then past the Crossroads Motel.

*Below:* The tall stone railway viaduct north of Devoran.

7. At the T-junction turn right then follow the road left across the bridge over the A30 (use the pavement/cyclepath). Turn first left (signposted 'Wheal Rose'), shortly afterwards left again (by a granite waymark and some grey concrete workshops), then after 50yd first right to rejoin the traffic-free trail.

8. Follow this good track gently downhill. At the end go straight ahead on to the lane opposite. At the crossroads of lanes go straight ahead.

9. At the next road turn left on to the light brown-coloured cyclepath alongside the road. After $^3/_4$ mile, at the end of the cyclepath, turn right to cross the road then immediately left. This soon becomes a gravel path.

10. Shortly after the end of a narrower section, at a fork bear right uphill (ie not left down towards the Bridge Inn which is on the main road). At the end of the path bear right on to a lane.

11. At the end of Sunnyvale Road emerge in Portreath by the Portreath Arms. For the harbour and beach continue straight ahead towards the hill.

# ST AUSTELL TO MEVAGISSEY
*(10 miles south of Bodmin)*

Although part of this route was included in the first volume of *Cycling Without Traffic: Southwest*, such is the pace of development of the National Cycle Network that a whole new section has been built since then. It forms part of the Cornish Way, the 180-mile cycle route that runs from Land's End to Bude. The traffic-free section starts in the woodland just south of St Austell and follows the river valley down towards the seaside village of Pentewan. After about a mile you have the choice of continuing on the flat towards the beach or climbing up past the Lost Gardens of Heligan and down the other side of the hill to the popular fishing village of Mevagissey. The descent to Mevagissey is quite steep so you may well prefer to walk up the hill on the way back. As you are surrounded by wildflowers and fine views this hardly constitutes hardship!

**Starting Points and Parking:**
1. **London Apprentice.** The car park in Shepherdshill Woods just off the B3273 about 2 miles south of St Austell (Grid Reference 008498). Follow the B3273 towards Mevagissey. Just after the hamlet of London Apprentice turn left, signposted 'Retail Leisure Warehouse'. Follow the lane round to the right and park in the woods on the left.
2. **Mevagissey.** Park in the main car park on the B3273 just north of Mevagissey and once on your bike(s) follow the road towards St Austell. Shortly after passing a petrol station on the left, turn left by a 'Heligan Bike Trail' signpost. The gradient steepens soon after the start of the traffic-free section.

**Distance:** 4 miles one way; 8 miles return.

**Map:** Ordnance Survey Landranger Sheet 204. The *Cornish Way Cycle Route Map* produced by Sustrans (£5.99) shows this

*Below:* The quaint fishing village of Mevagissey.

*Above right:* The vast biospheres of the nearby Eden Project.

**Surface:** Good quality stone and gravel track.

**Roads and Road Crossings:** The B3273 is crossed via a traffic island near to Nansladron. If you wish to go right into the heart of Mevagissey you will need to use the road for about ½ mile.

**Refreshments:** Plenty of choice in Mevagissey and in Pentewan (there is also a traffic-free spur to the route down the Pentewan Valley to the coast).

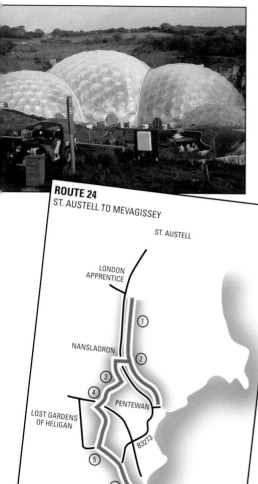

**ROUTE 24**
**ST. AUSTELL TO MEVAGISSEY**

ST. AUSTELL

LONDON APPRENTICE

NANSLADRON

① ② ③ ④

PENTEWAN

LOST GARDENS OF HELIGAN

B3273

⑤ ⑥

MEVAGISSEY

N

ROUTE INSTRUCTIONS:
1. From the car park in Shepherdshill Woods (near to the Retail Leisure Warehouse), follow the narrow tarmac lane through the woods. As the road swings left uphill, bear right on to the lower, broad woodland track.

2. The track runs alongside the river. After about 1 mile, at a bridge and a Millennium Milepost, you have a choice: straight on for Pentewan (1 mile) or turn right across the bridge for Mevagissey (3 miles).

3. (Towards Mevagissey.) After crossing the bridge, turn left at the road (B3273) along the shared-use pavement. Cross the road via the traffic island and continue alongside the road. The track swings right, away from the road and soon begins to climb.

4. The track climbs steadily. At a junction of tracks, shortly after a zigzag, turn right for Mevagissey (or go straight ahead for the Lost Gardens of Heligan – this will involve about ½ mile along a fairly busy road).

5. (Mevagissey.) Descend, climb, then descend again. At the T-junction (with a footpath to the left) turn right. A steep descent follows.

6. The track ends at the road on the edge of Mevagissey. Turn right to visit this popular fishing village. Retrace your route.

and several other traffic-free routes in Cornwall including the Camel Trail, the Mineral Tramroad from Bissoe to Devoran and the route through Penzance from Mousehole to Marazion.

**Hills:** There is a long 300ft climb from the Pentewan Valley up towards Heligan Gardens then a long descent to Mevagissey.

## ALONG CHALK TRACKS FROM RINGSTEAD BAY TO WEST LULWORTH
*(5 miles east of Weymouth)*

Of all the counties covered by this book, Dorset and Wiltshire have the densest network of bridleways and byways where it is both possible and legal to ride offroad. The quality of the tracks can vary significantly from winter to summer and prolonged rain at any time of the year will make the ground softer and muddier. This said, there are some excellent routes along the chalk ridges, both on the coast and inland. These are not cycle trails in the sense of converted railways or Forestry Commission land but as a taste of real 'off-road' riding they offer some exhilarating cycling and magnificent views. This one has the added bonus of fine sea views.

*Below:* Rolling chalk tracks through Dorset.

**Starting Point and Parking:** Take the (easily missed) minor road off the A353 between Weymouth and the A352, signposted 'Ringstead'. If you are coming from Weymouth, it is the next right **after** the right turn to Osmington Mills. If you are coming from the A352 and you get to Osmington you will know that you have come too far and should return 1 mile along the A353. Once you have found the minor road, keep bearing left and follow it for 1½ miles to the National Trust car park.

**Distance:** 5 miles one way; 10 miles return.

**Map:** Ordnance Survey Landranger Sheet 194.

**Hills:** One long and steady climb of 165ft (50m) in the first half of the ride, and several shorter climbs. On the return, the longest climb is from West Lulworth up the minor road to the start of the track at Daggers Gate.

**Surface:** Chalk and stone; smooth grass; short rough field-edge sections; tarmac road from Daggers Gate to West Lulworth. Mountain bikes only. Best done after a few dry days in the summer months (May to September). There will be mud in the winter and after prolonged rain.

**Roads and Road Crossings:** A 1½-mile section of road is used down into West Lulworth. This will take less than 5 minutes to go down but closer to 15 minutes on the way up as it involves almost 300ft of climbing.

**Refreshments:** Lots of choice in West Lulworth.

ROUTE INSTRUCTIONS:
1. Continue to the far end of the car park, go through the gate and keep following the broad chalk and flint track.

2. Descend then bear left to pass through a metal/wooden fieldgate on to the track, which leads to the left of the house and the thatched barn.

*Above:* The fascinating rock formation of Durdle Door. *Dorset Tourism*

*Left:* The Tank Museum. *Dorset Tourism*

3. Climb, pass through a metal gate (one of two gates, side by side). Continue in the same direction along a much rougher and grassier track. Emerge into a pasture cropped by livestock.

4. Follow the fence/wall on the left and signs for Daggers Gate and Lulworth. At the T-junction with the road at the bottom of a fast descent, turn right. (Remember this point for the return trip.)

5. Follow this downhill for 1½ miles into West Lulworth and refreshments. Retrace your steps (you may wish to push your bike up the pavement alongside the road on the climb back up to the chalk and flint track).

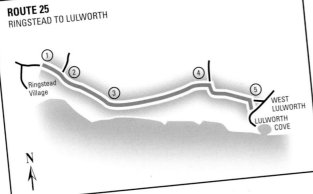

**ROUTE 25**
RINGSTEAD TO LULWORTH

Ringstead Village

WEST LULWORTH

LULWORTH COVE

N

## AFFPUDDLE HEATH FORESTRY
*(7 miles east of Dorchester)*

The eastern half of Dorset becomes increasingly wooded as the chalklands of the western half give way to sandier soils more appropriate for growing coniferous trees, culminating in the New Forest. These first outliers of coniferous woodland give a taste of the joys of broad, stone-based forest roads that can be ridden year-round without fear of thick mud or rough and rutted surfaces. The open heathland between the trees is carpeted with brightly coloured gorse and heather. Getting lost in woodland without full waymarking is always a possibility but as you are never far away from roads and villages this will not really be as bad as it sounds!

*Right:* Mixed heathland and woodland makes this ride a real delight.

**Starting Point and Parking:** The Culpeppers Dish Forestry Commission car park to the south of Briantspuddle at Grid Reference 815924. Turn off the A35 dual carriageway on to the B3390 (about 8 miles east of Dorchester) towards Affpuddle. Almost a mile after passing through the hamlet of Affpuddle take the next road to the left. The car park is about ¾ mile along on the right.

**Distance:** 5-mile circuit.

**Map:** Ordnance Survey Landranger Sheet 194.

**Hills:** Several gentle hills. The route is mainly downhill on the first half of the ride and uphill on the way back.

**Surface:** Generally broad, stone-based forest roads. Mountain bikes recommended.

**Roads and Road Crossings:** There are two short sections on road. The first road (at the start and finish of the ride) is fairly quiet; the other road (used for about 300yd) carries more traffic and care should be taken.

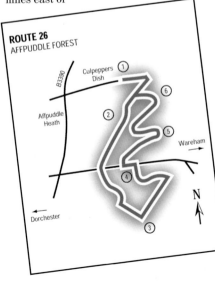

ROUTE INSTRUCTIONS:

1. Leave the car park, following yellow cycle arrows (just to the right of the big wooden arch over the Play Trail entrance). The trail starts along tarmac then turns left at a 'Castleman Trailway' sign.

2. At the T-junction at the end turn left, signposted 'Castleman Trailway, Tree Top Trail'. Shortly after passing a stag beetle wooden sculpture on the right and just before a left turn to the Tree Top Trail you have a choice: straight ahead to return to the Visitor Centre (follow the yellow waymarks) or turn right for the full route (follow blue waymarks).

3. (Full Route.) Follow the trail around a left-hand bend, climb gently then at the T-junction turn right.

*Above:* Dappled woodland sunlight falls on heather and ferns.

4. A gentle descent is followed by a gentle climb. At the next T-junction turn left and shortly afterwards turn left again, with the road close by to the right.

5. At a four-way signpost you have a choice: go straight ahead to return to the Visitor Centre (the yellow waymarks) or turn right for the full route (the lilac waymarks, shortly turning left at a crossroads near to the road).

6. After $3/4$ mile, at a T-junction turn left, signposted 'Lookout'. Enjoy the longest and fastest descent of the day.

7. At the T-junction at the bottom of the hill you have a choice: turn left for the Visitor Centre (the yellow waymarks) or turn right for the full route (the red waymarks).

8. (Full Route.) Shortly afterwards take the first left by a holly tree and a wooden bench (red waymark). Descend to cross a wooden bridge and soon afterwards turn right to cross a second bridge.

9. Follow the trail through the golf course and over several wiremesh-covered wooden walkways. At a tall signpost turn right over a wooden bridge past the steam railway back to the Visitor Centre.

## NEW FOREST CIRCUIT NEAR LINWOOD
*(3 miles northeast of Ringwood)*

There are hundreds of miles of tracks in the New Forest, a wonderful asset, but they do not all link up easily; the real target when going for a bike ride in the area is to minimise the time spent on tarmac, as even the minor roads can get very busy with traffic, particularly on fine summer weekends. This ride on the northwestern edge of the New Forest just about fulfils all the right criteria and throws in a fine country pub for good measure. The suggested starting point is on the edge of the woodland of Milkham Inclosure but as there are several car parks in the area and the route is circular it could be joined elsewhere. The ride starts with a long gentle woodland descent following the valley formed by Linford Brook, climbs to the road, goes past the Red Shoot Inn and soon plunges back into woodland. A wide expanse of heather is crossed near Broomy Plain before rejoining the road briefly to return to the start and complete the circuit.

**Starting Point and Parking:** The Milkham Inclosure car park at Grid Reference 218104. This is on the minor road that passes through Linwood, to the northeast of Ringwood. If coming from Ringwood, go north on the minor road towards Rockford and South Gorley and follow the road through Linwood towards Fritham. About 2 miles after passing the Red Shoot Inn at Linwood, turn right on the gravel track into Milkham car park (opposite a road turning on the left).

**Distance:** 5-mile circuit.

**Map:** Ordnance Survey Landranger Sheet 195.

**Hills:** Several gentle hills.

**Surface:** Good stone-based tracks.

**Roads and Road Crossings:** There are two short road sections – the first either side of the Red Shoot Inn and the second at the end of the ride to return to the car park.

**Refreshments:** The Red Shoot Inn, Linwood.

*Below:* The Red Shoot Inn is a popular watering hole for thirsty cyclists.

ROUTE INSTRUCTIONS:

1. From the Milkham Inclosure car park take the track leading directly away from the road through the gate. Shortly after a crossroads with a rough wide track, bear left downhill on the main broad gravel track for a long descent. Keep bearing left.

2. At the bottom of the hill at a T-junction by a cycle signpost with a three-way arrow marked '5', turn right through the narrow barrier over the bridge. The track climbs.

3. Emerge at the road and turn left downhill for about ½ mile. Turn right to go past the Red Shoot Inn. Follow the no through road as it turns to track. At the first fork (with a thatched cottage to the right) bear left.

4. **Ignore** several turnings into private properties to the left and right. At the end of these properties, turn left by a wooden barrier with a three-way cycle arrow.

5. Go through two gates (with adjacent bridlegates). At the first major crossroads of broad, stone forest roads, by a cycle signpost marked '3', turn right (past Holly Hatch Cottage) and start to climb.

6. Emerge at the road and bear left (in effect, straight ahead). After ¼ mile, opposite a road turn to the left, turn right to return to the Milkham car park.

*Above:* The New Forest has as much open space as woodland.

*Below:* Lush vegetation lines the woodland tracks.

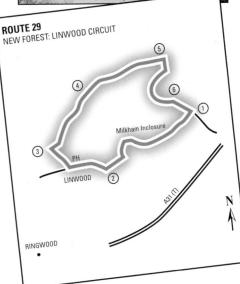

ROUTE 29
NEW FOREST: LINWOOD CIRCUIT

Milkham Inclosure

LINWOOD

PH

RINGWOOD

A31 (T)

N

## THE NEW FOREST RAILWAY PATH, NEAR BURLEY

*(4 miles southeast of Ringwood)*

Within the context of the vast cycling opportunities of the New Forest it may seem a little strange to be using a railway path, more associated with traffic-free cycling in areas of the country less blessed with forestry and heathland tracks. However, railway paths have the distinct advantage of going in a straight line and allowing for no chance of getting lost! The only drawback on this splendid path across the open heathland, once the London & South Western Railway branch line via Ringwood to Brockenhurst, is the fact that the middle section has been covered in tarmac and is now used as a road. It is a shame that a parallel path for cyclists was not built at the same time as the road. This means you can either do the two traffic-free sections (of 2 and 3 miles) separately or you can link them together by using the road section, which can be busy in the height of the season.

*Left:* The old railway is now a broad avenue of trees.

'there-and-back' traffic-free rides of 4 miles or 6 miles **OR** a 13-mile there-and-back ride which will involve a road section in the middle.

**Map:** Ordnance Survey Landranger Sheet 195.

**Hills:** There are a few short, sharp climbs where bridges have been removed and you need to climb back up on to the embankment.

**Starting Points and Parking:**
1. Burbush Hill car park, about 1 mile southwest of Burley on the road towards Bransgore (Grid Reference 202018). Soon after the end of the houses in Burley, turn left into the car park just **before** the metal bridge.
2. Wootton Coppice Inclosure car park, on the minor road that runs northeast from the B3058 (to the north of New Milton) to Brockenhurst (Grid Reference 250997).
3. Longslade Bottom car park, about 1 mile north of Sway (Grid Reference 270002).

**Distance:** There are two traffic-free railway path sections – one of 2 miles (in the west) and the other of 3 miles (in the east). These two sections are connected by a 1½-mile road section. So you have a choice of two

**Surface:** Good-quality stone and gravel track. Short sections may become muddy in the winter and after prolonged rain. Mountain bikes or hybrids are recommended.

**Roads and Road Crossings:** If you choose to link the two traffic-free sections by using the connecting road you will have to ride for about 1½ miles on tarmac. As with all the roads and lanes in the New Forest, this

NEW FOREST

🌳 Forestry Commission

We are Protecting the Crown Lands of the New Forest. We put the Forest First for the benefit of wildlife and people alike

one can be busy in the height of the summer. **TAKE CARE.** If, however, you choose to split the railway path into two separate rides you do not need to spend any time on roads.

**Refreshments:** The Old Station Tea Rooms at the point where the railway/minor road passes beneath the A35. Otherwise, there is plenty of choice in Burley.

ROUTE INSTRUCTIONS:
1. Go to the far end of Burbush Hill car park and exit to the right on to the railway path, following bike signs. Go past the ruins of a large red-brick bridge.

2. At the crossroads with a minor road go straight ahead. The first traffic-free section ends at the Old Station Tea Rooms. You can either turn around here or, if you wish to link with the other section, you will need to spend 1½ miles on road. If you choose to go on, remember this point well for your return as it is easily missed on the way back.

3. (Full route.) At the T-junction with the road turn left then immediately right at the

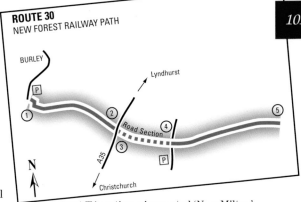

**ROUTE 30**
NEW FOREST RAILWAY PATH

BURLEY

Lyndhurst

P

1

2

Road Section

4

3

A35

P

5

N

Christchurch

next T-junction, signposted 'New Milton'. Pass beneath the bridge.

4. After about 1½ miles, as the road swings round to the left, take the first road to the right by a triangle of grass then turn left on to a track. This rejoins the railway path.

5. Pass beneath a road bridge. Descend and climb back up on to the track at the two missing bridges. Go past a small white house with a tall chimney. The trail ends at the B3055, near to its junction with the railway. Retrace your route.

*Below:* New Forest ponies graze oblivious to passing cyclists.

## A. ROUTES DESCRIBED IN THE FIRST *CYCLING WITHOUT TRAFFIC: SOUTHWEST*

The 30 routes below are described more fully in the first *Cycling Without Traffic: Southwest*, also published by Dial House, available from all good bookshops.

1. The Newport to Cowes Cycleway, Isle of Wight.
2. The Test Way from Stonymarsh to Stockbridge, west of Winchester.
3.. Denny Circular Route, northeast of Brockenhurst, New Forest.
4. Burley Circular Route, north of Burley, New Forest.
5. Fritham Circular Route, northwest of Lyndhurst, New Forest.
6. The Marlborough to Chiseldon Railway Path, south of Swindon.
7. The Kennet & Avon Canal Towpath from Pewsey to Devizes.
8. The Salisbury Way from Wilton to Fovant, west of Salisbury.
9. Grovely Wood Roman Road from Wilton to Wylye, west of Salisbury.
10. The Castleman Trailway from Moors Valley Country Park to West Moors, southwest of Ringwood.
11. The Castleman Trailway from Wimborne Minster to Upton Country Park (north of Poole).
12. The Kennet & Avon Canal Towpath from Devizes to Hilperton.
13. The Imber Range Perimeter Path, east of Westbury, Wiltshire.
14. The Fosse Way, southwest of Malmesbury (to the west of Swindon).
15. The Kennet & Avon Canal Towpath from Bath to Bradford on Avon.
16. The Bristol & Bath Railway Path.
17. On the hills around Dorchester, South Dorset.
18. The Axbridge to Cheddar Cycleway (southwest of Bristol).
19. The Bridgwater & Taunton Canal Towpath from Bridgwater to Lower Maunsel.
20. The Bridgwater & Taunton Canal Towpath from Taunton to Lower Maunsel.

21. Eggesford Forest, northwest of Exeter.
22. Princetown and Burrator Circular Route, Dartmoor National Park.
23. The Plym Valley Cycle Trail, north of Plymouth.
24. The Tarka Trail from Petrockstowe to East-the-Water, Bideford, North Devon.
25. The Cairn & Old Railway Path from Ilfracombe to Lee Bridge, North Devon.
26. The Tarka Trail from East-the-Water to Barnstaple, North Devon.
27. The Camel Trail from Poley's Bridge to Wadebridge, Cornwall.
28. The Pentewan Valley Leisure Trail, south of St Austell, Cornwall.
29. The Camel Trail from Wadebridge to Padstow, Cornwall.
30. The Portreath Tramroad, north of Camborne, Cornwall.

# B. OTHER ROUTES IN BRIEF

*In addition to the main rides described in this book and the trails described in the first volume of* Cycling Without Traffic: Southwest, *there are several shorter trails (less than 3 miles) which may be worth exploring if they happen to lie close to where you live. Many of these will form part of the National Cycle Network and are likely to be further developed as time goes on.*

## Bristol
1. St Philips Greenway from Temple Meads to Whitchurch. Starts on Cattle Market Road and follows the River Avon (the southern section is in development).

## Cornwall
1. Penzance to Marazion. There is a 2-mile cyclepath alongside the railway line between Penzance railway station and Marazion.
2. Idless Woods, north of Truro.

## Dorset
1. The Rodwell Trail from Weymouth towards Portland. Starts at the roundabout in Weymouth at the junction of the A353 and A354 and runs south towards Portland Bill.
2. Puddletown Forest, east of Dorchester.

## Devon
1. Elburton to Yealmpton Railway Path (east of Plymouth). Starts at the A379 on the eastern edge of Plymouth. (In development.)
2. The Tiverton Railway Path east from Tiverton. Starts near the junction of the A396 with the Halberton Road.
3. Shortacombe, Dartmoor. A tough 4-mile tramway that climbs almost 800ft up from the Fox & Hounds PH on the A386, about 7 miles southwest of Okehampton.
4. Haldon Forest (southwest of Exeter).
5. Forestry at Soussons and Fernworthy (on Dartmoor).

## Somerset (including Bath & North East Somerset, North Somerset)
1. Langport – a 1½-mile stretch of railway path running south of Langport.

*Below:* The Forest of Dean Family Trail.

It starts just to the west of the bridge over the River Parrett.

2. Wells – a short railway path which follows the West Country Way from the Bishop's Palace east to Dulcote.
3. The grassy bridleway which runs along the ridge of the Mendips to Crook Peak. Follow the bridleway west from King's Wood, starting at the car park off the A38 (located 1 mile south of Winscombe). This ride involves some steep climbs.
4. Radstock to Midsomer Norton. A 2-mile railway path starting from the western edge of Radstock, at a small car park just off the A362.
5. Winscombe railway path. Runs south from Winscombe parallel with the A38. Could easily be linked to the Axbridge–Cheddar railway path.

### Wiltshire

1. Newbury (Berkshire) – Kennet & Avon Canal towpath west from Newbury to Marsh Benham.
2. Woodland near Marlborough – Savernake (permissive) and West Woods.
3. Swindon Old Town Railway Path.
4. Coate Water Country Park, on the southeast edge of Swindon.
5. There are several sections of the Ridgeway (other than the first part which is described in Ride 10) which are worth exploring on a fine summer's day after a good long dry spell.

## C. FORESTRY COMMISSION LAND

The Southwest of England is not nearly as forested as Wales or Scotland or even the Southeast of England. There are nevertheless two large forestry holdings, the New Forest and the Forest of Dean, where there are many miles of waymarked trails. There are some smaller holdings which have waymarked trails, others where I have described routes for you to follow, and others still where it is possible to devise your own route. (See below under A, B and C.)

The Forestry Commission has, by and large, adopted an enlightened approach to cycling in its woodlands. The broad rule of thumb is that you are welcome to use the hard, stone-based forestry roads which provide excellent opportunities for safe, family cycling. In certain woodlands there are also waymarked trails on 'single track' paths which are often more testing. You should pay attention to any signs which may indicate a temporary or permanent restriction on cycling (normally on walkers' trails or where forestry operations are in progress).

The best maps to use for exploring Forestry Commission woodland are the most up-to-date Ordnance Survey maps.

PLEASE NOTE: It must be stressed that there are many different user groups enjoying the woodlands, so courtesy and

*Left:* Big Dartmoor views from Bellever Forest.

consideration should be shown at all times to walkers and horse riders. The fact that a bike can travel faster than a pedestrian does not give you any priority; indeed priority normally lies with the walker or the horse rider. Use a bell or say 'Hello' to give warning of your presence and thank people who step aside for you.

A. FORESTRY WITH WAYMARKED
   TRAILS
There are five Forestry Commission holdings with waymarked trails in the area:
1. The Forest of Dean, Gloucestershire (Route 2, page 22).
2. Eggesford Forest, 20 miles northwest of Exeter (covered in the first *Cycling Without Traffic: Southwest*).
3. Dunster Woods, south of Minehead, Exmoor (Route 12, page 52).
4. Moors Valley Country Park, on the Dorset/Hampshire border near Ringwood (Route 28, page 96).
5. The New Forest. There are an infinite number of routes in what is the largest forestry holding in England south of Yorkshire. Three routes are described in the first *Cycling Without Traffic: Southwest*. Two further rides are described in this book: Route 29 (page 98) and Route 30 (page 100).

B. OTHER FORESTRY AREAS WITH
   ROUTES DESCRIBED IN THIS BOOK
1. Abbeyford Woods (Route 16, page 64).
2. Bellever Forest, Dartmoor (Route 19, page 72).
3. Cardinham Woods, east of Bodmin (Route 22, page 82).
4. Affpuddle Heath (Route 26, page 92).
5. Wareham Forest (Route 27, page 94).

C. OTHER FORESTRY HOLDINGS
   (NEITHER WAYMARKED NOR
   DESCRIBED)
In addition to the waymarked forestry trails listed above there are other forestry holdings throughout the Southwest where it would be possible to devise your own routes on the forestry roads. Here are a few

suggestions together with the appropriate Ordnance Survey Landranger map:
1. The Wye Valley between Chepstow and Monmouth (OS 162).
2. Collingbourne and West Woods, southwest and south of Marlborough (OS 173 and 184).
3. Quantocks woodland, west of Bridgwater (OS 181).
4. Dartmoor: Soussons and Fernworthy, between Princetown and Moretonhampstead (OS 191).
5. Haldon, southwest of Exeter (OS 191 and 192).
6. Idless Woods, north of Truro (OS 204).
7. Other woodland north and west of Bodmin: Dunmere, Great Grogley and Hustyn (OS 200).
8. Puddletown Forest, east of Dorchester (OS 194).
9. Isle of Purbeck, northeast of Corfe Castle, Dorset (OS 195).

The best publication showing all these holdings is a 48-page A4 booklet called *Ramblers' Atlas of Public Forests* published by the Ramblers' Association. It is available free from: Ramblers' Association, 2nd Floor, Camelford House, 87-90 Albert Embankment, London SE1 7PW. This together with the appropriate Ordnance Survey Landranger (1:50,000) or Explorer (1:25,000) map will allow you to see your options and plan your routes.

Contact the following Forest Enterprise District Offices for further information:

Forest of Dean
Bank House, Bank Street, Coleford,
Gloucestershire GL16 8BA
Tel: 01594 833057

Peninsula Forest District
(Devon and Cornwall)
Bullers Hill, Kennford, Exeter,
Devon EX6 7XR
Tel: 01392 832262

New Forest
The Queens House, Lyndhurst,
Hampshire SO43 7NH
Tel: 023 8028 3141

## D. CANAL TOWPATHS AND REGIONAL WATERWAYS BOARDS

The theory is that there are 2,000 miles of towpaths in England and Wales, offering flat, vehicle-free cycling. The reality is that only a fraction of the towpath network is suitable for cycling: the rest is too narrow, overgrown, muddy and rough. There is obviously much room for improvement and certain Waterway Boards, in conjunction with local authorities and the Countryside Agency, have made immense progress in improving towpaths for all user groups. However, even the areas which have a reasonable surface are often busy with anglers and walkers, so when cycling on canal towpaths, extra care and consideration are needed.

Within the book there are three rides on sections of canal towpaths (others were covered in the first *Cycling Without Traffic: Southwest*). For the rest of the canal network please refer to the addresses and phone numbers of the local Waterways Board covering your area. There is no overall guideline about cycling on towpaths: some authorities issue a permit and charge for it; others issue a free permit; some have opened up the whole towpath to cyclists; others allow cycling only on certain sections. The most up-to-date information can be obtained from your local Waterways Board.

The addresses and phone numbers are as follows:

- British Waterways, The Wharf, Govilon, Abergavenny NP7 9NY
  Tel: 01873 830328
  Covers the Bridgwater & Taunton Canal and the Monmouthshire & Brecon Canal. The Bridgwater & Taunton Canal, linking those two towns, was described in the first *Cycling Without Traffic: Southwest*.

- British Waterways, Llanthony Warehouse, Gloucester Docks, Gloucester GL1 2EJ
  Tel: 01452 318000
  Covers the Gloucester & Sharpness Canal.

- British Waterways, The Locks, Bath Road, Devizes, Wiltshire SN10 1HB
  Tel: 01380 722859
  Covers the Kennet & Avon Canal between Bath and Reading.

Although the two canals running north from Newport in South Wales lie just outside the area covered, they are worthy of mention as they offer excellent cycling. Both form an integral part of the National Cycle Network: one runs north to Pontypool then joins a railway path up to Blaenavon; the other runs northwest towards Crosskeys to join the railway path through Sirhowy Valley Country Park. The best starting point for both Newport rides is the Visitor Centre at Fourteen Locks to the north of M4 Jct 27 (west of Newport).

## THE WATERWAYS CODE FOR CYCLISTS

- Avoid cycling where your tyres would damage the path or verges (eg when they are wet or soft).
- Give way to others on the towpath and warn them of your approach. A polite 'Hello' and 'Thankyou' mean a lot.
- Dismount under low or blind bridges and where the path is very narrow.
- Never race one another or perform speed trials.
- We recommend you obtain third party liability insurance and equip your bike with a bell or equivalent.
- Access paths can be steep and slippery. Join or leave the towpath with care.
- Take special care if cycling at night. Use front and rear lights.
- Watch out when passing moored boats – there may be mooring spikes concealed on the path.

*Right:* The National Cycle Network uses a mixture of traffic-free paths and quiet lanes.

# E. SUSTRANS' NATIONAL CYCLE NETWORK

The National Cycle Network is a linked series of traffic-free paths and traffic-calmed roads being developed right across the United Kingdom, joining town centres and the countryside. June 2000 saw the opening of the first 5,000 miles and a further 5,000 miles will open by 2005.

For more information about Sustrans and the National Cycle Network contact Sustrans' Information Service on 0117 929 0888 or visit its website at www.nationalcyclenetwork.org.uk. Maps covering the routes described below are sold by Sustrans.

In the region covered by this book there are three long sections of the National Cycle Network that have been opened so far:

### 1. The Cornish Way/West Country Way

National Route 3 runs from the very tip of the British mainland at Land's End up to Bristol and Bath. It links some of the most well-known traffic-free trails in the region – the Camel Trail near Bodmin, the Tarka Trail near Barnstaple, the Bridgwater & Taunton Canal towpath and the Bristol & Bath Railway Path. All of these were covered in the first *Cycling Without Traffic: Southwest*.

Other traffic-free sections which have opened more recently are covered in this book either as main routes or in the 'Other Routes in Brief' section:
1. The Mineral Tramroad to the east of Redruth (Route 23).
2. St Austell to Pentewan and Mevagissey (Route 24).
3. Grand Western Canal northeast of Tiverton (Route 15).
4. Willow Walk to the west of Glastonbury (Route 14).
5. Penzance: from Mousehole to Marazion ('Other Routes in Brief').

### 2. The Devon Coast to Coast

Crossing Devon from Plymouth on the south coast to Ilfracombe on the north, this route starts and finishes with traffic-free trails: the Plym Valley Path runs from Laira Bridge on the east side of Plymouth up to Clearbrook; at its northern end, a long section of the Tarka Trail is enjoyed before the finish along a railway path from Lee Bridge into Ilfracombe. All three rides are described in the first *Cycling Without Traffic: Southwest*. In the middle part of the route Sustrans has been busy around Okehampton, opening up the spectacular Meldon Viaduct (Route 17). There are also plans to create a safe link from the southern end of the Tarka Tail to Hatherleigh and work will continue around Tavistock to increase the proportion of traffic-free route.

### 3. The Severn & Thames Cycle Route

This 'L'-shaped route heads south from Gloucester to Bristol then east through Bath towards Newbury and Reading. Along its first section it uses the Gloucester & Sharpness Canal towpath (Route 3) and the Bristol to Pill Riverside Path (Route 7). The Bristol & Bath Railway Path and the Kennet & Avon Canal towpath are described in the first *Cycling Without Traffic: Southwest*. In the last couple of years, new sections have been built or massively improved between Chippenham and Calne (Route 9) and along the canal to the west of Newbury (see 'Other Routes in Brief').

## LOCAL AUTHORITY LEAFLETS

Local authorities often produce cycling leaflets, such as town maps showing urban cycle networks or leaflets describing recreational routes in the countryside. However, when trying to obtain these leaflets, do not expect any logic or consistency: not only does the quantity and quality of leaflets vary from one authority to the next but each authority seems to have a different name for the department in charge of cycling! In addition, some charge for their leaflets and some give them away free. Just to complicate matters further, local authorities are forever reorganising and changing department names, then of course leaflets run out and are not reprinted...

As you can see it would be very easy to give information that would be out of date almost as soon as the book is published, so instead we are suggesting that *you* become the detective and find out from your own local authority what cycling leaflets it has produced. Below is a list of the main telephone numbers of each of the local authorities (County Councils, Metropolitan Councils, Unitary Authorities) in the area covered by this book.

When you call, ask to speak to 'The Cycling Officer' or to someone about recreational or family cycling. You may be put through to one of the following departments: Planning, Highways, Tourism, Transport, Environment, Access & Recreation or the Countryside Section and do not be surprised to be transferred from one department to another! Have a pen and paper handy so that when you *do* get through to the right person you can note down his or her name and direct phone line and the address to which you should send money (if required). This person may also be able to help you with the names of people to speak to in the adjoining authorities.

An alternative to this is to contact Sustrans Information Service, PO Box 21, Bristol BS99 2HA (Tel: 0117 929 0888). For a small handling fee Sustrans should be able to provide you with the leaflets you require.

Why not visit the Sustrans website at www.nationalcyclenetwork.org.uk

# TOURIST INFORMATION CENTRES

Another option in your quest for further cycling information is to contact the Tourist Information Centre(s) covering the area in which you are interested. They frequently stock local leaflets and booklets that don't find their way into bookshops or any form of national distribution. The telephone numbers of the Tourist Information Centres in the larger towns and cities are listed below.

| Town | Telephone number | E-mail address |
| --- | --- | --- |
| Barnstaple | 01271 375000 | (e-mail not available) |
| Bath | 01225 477101 | bath_tourism@bathnes.gov.uk |
| Bideford | 01237 477676 | bidefordtic@visit.org.uk |
| Bodmin | 01208 76616 | bodmintic@visit.org.uk |
| Bournemouth | 01202 451700 | info@bournemouth.gov.uk |
| Bridgwater | 01278 427652 | bridgwater.tic@sedgemoor.gov.uk |
| Bristol | 0117 926 0767 | bristol@tourism.bristol.gov.uk |
| Cheltenham | 01242 522878 | tic@cheltenham.gov.uk |
| Chippenham | 01249 706333 | tourism@northwilts.gov.uk |
| Cirencester | 01285 654180 | (e-mail not available) |
| Dorchester | 01305 267992 | tourism@westdorset-dc.gov.uk |
| Exeter | 01392 265700 | tic@exeter.gov.uk |
| Exmouth | 01395 222299 | (e-mail not available) |
| Falmouth | 01326 312300 | falmouthtic@yahoo.co.uk |
| Glastonbury | 01458 832954 | glastonbury.tic@ukonline.co.uk |
| Gloucester | 01452 421188 | tourism@gloscity.gov.uk |
| Marlborough | 01672 513989 | (e-mail not available) |
| Minehead | 01643 702624 | mineheadtic@visit.org.uk |
| Okehampton | 01837 53020 | oketic@visit.org.uk |
| Penzance | 01736 362207 | (e-mail not available) |
| Plymouth | 01752 304849 | plymouthbarbicantic@visit.org.uk |
| Salisbury | 01722 334956 | salisburytic@salisbury.gov.uk |
| Stroud | 01453 760960 | tic@stroud.gov.uk |
| Swindon | 01793 530328 | infocentre@swindon.gov.uk |
| Taunton | 01823 336344 | tautic@somerset.gov.uk |
| Tavistock | 01822 612938 | tavistocktic@visit.org.uk |
| Truro | 01872 274555 | (e-mail not available) |
| Yeovil | 01935 471279 | yeoviltic@southsomerset.gov.uk |

## LOCAL AUTHORITIES' TELEPHONE NUMBERS AND WEBSITES

| Authority | Telephone number | Website address |
|---|---|---|
| Bath & North East Somerset | 01225 477000 | (website not available) |
| Bournemouth | 01202 451451 | www.bournemouth.gov.uk |
| Bristol City Council | 0117 922 2000 | www.bristol-city.gov.uk |
| Cornwall | 01872 322000 | (website not available) |
| Devon | 01392 382000 | www.devon-cc.gov.uk |
| Dorset | 01305 251000 | www.dorset-cc.gov.uk |
| Gloucestershire | 01452 425000 | www.gloscc.gov.uk |
| Hampshire | 01962 841841 | www.hants.gov.uk |
| Herefordshire | 01432 260000 | www.herefordshire.gov.uk |
| North Somerset | 01934 888888 | (website not available) |
| Oxfordshire | 01865 815246 | www.oxfordshire.gov.uk |
| Plymouth City Council | 01752 668000 | www.plymouth.gov.uk |
| Poole | 01202 633706 | (website not available) |
| Somerset | 01823 355455 | www.somerset.gov.uk |
| South Gloucestershire | 01454 868686 | www.southglos.gov.uk |
| Swindon | 01793 463000 | www.swindon.gov.uk |
| Torbay | 01803 201201 | www.torbay.gov.uk |
| West Berkshire | 01635 42400 | www.westberks.gov.uk |
| Wiltshire | 01225 713000 | (website not available) |

*This page:* A lovely track in Abbeyford Woods, near Okehampton.

*Above left:* Sun, sea, sand and ... cycling!